Cambridge Elements ≡

Elements in the Philosophy of Science
edited by
Jacob Stegenga
University of Cambridge

OBJECTIVITY IN SCIENCE

Stephen John
University of Cambridge

CAMBRIDGE
UNIVERSITY PRESS

University Printing House, Cambridge CB2 8BS, United Kingdom

One Liberty Plaza, 20th Floor, New York, NY 10006, USA

477 Williamstown Road, Port Melbourne, VIC 3207, Australia

314–321, 3rd Floor, Plot 3, Splendor Forum, Jasola District Centre, New Delhi – 110025, India

79 Anson Road, #06–04/06, Singapore 079906

Cambridge University Press is part of the University of Cambridge.

It furthers the University's mission by disseminating knowledge in the pursuit of education, learning, and research at the highest international levels of excellence.

www.cambridge.org
Information on this title: www.cambridge.org/9781009065337
DOI: 10.1017/9781009063647

First published 2021

A catalogue record for this publication is available from the British Library.

ISBN 978-1-009-06533-7 Paperback
ISSN 2517-7273 (online)
ISSN 2517-7265 (print)

Objectivity in Science

Elements in the Philosophy of Science

DOI: 10.1017/9781009063647
First published online: May 2021

Stephen John
University of Cambridge

Author for correspondence: Stephen John, sdj22@cam.ac.uk

Abstract: Objectivity is a key concept both in how we talk about science in everyday life and in the philosophy of science. This Element explores various ways in which recent philosophers of science have thought about the nature, value and achievability of objectivity. The first section explains the general trend in recent philosophy of science away from a notion of objectivity as a 'view from nowhere' to a focus on the relationship between objectivity and trust. Section 2 discusses the relationship between objectivity and recent arguments attacking the viability or desirability of 'value free' science. Section 3 outlines Longino's influential 'social' account of objectivity, suggesting some worries about drawing too strong a link between epistemic and ethical virtues. Section 4 turns to the value of objectivity, exploring concerns that notions of objectivity are politically problematic, and cautiously advocating in response a view of objectivity in terms of invariance.

Keywords: philosophy of science, objectivity, bias, trust, values in science

ISBNs: 9781009065337 (PB), 9781009063647 (OC)
ISSNs: 2517-7273 (online), 2517-7265 (print)

Contents

1 Objectivity: Processes and Products

Consider some quotations from recent news articles:

> [The court's judgment] gives judicial licence for women and men who speak up for objective truth and clear debate to be subject to aggression, bullying, no-platforming and economic punishment (Bowcott, 2019).
>
> When presented with lies versus truth, every journalist is facing a test of conscience. Are you being truly objective and just or are you being selective and partial? What does your decision reveal? TRUTH AIN'T LIE! (Kuo, 2019).
>
> Teachers, particularly of the sciences, have smuggled political positions into what should be factual and objective subjects (Seaman, 2019).

All three of these quotes vividly convey a sense that it is important to be 'objective' – to speak up for objective truth, to engage in objective journalism or to maintain the objectivity of teaching – but, also, that objectivity is fragile, and under attack. In turn, they relate to broader social worries that we are moving into a post-truth world, dominated by 'fake news' and a disregard for science and rationality. But they are puzzling: they suggest that certain things – selectivity, partiality, political commitments – *threaten* objectivity, but is there anything *more* to objectivity than the absence of these factors? To complicate matters further, all three quotes arise in the context of heated ongoing debates. The first quote is a response to a ruling over transgender rights; the second is from China's Ministry of Foreign Affairs, berating coverage of China's domestic policies; and the third is from a climate sceptic, decrying the teaching of climate science in schools. Can talk of objectivity really resolve politically charged debates, or is it just a mask for social and political agendas?

There is an obvious response to these concerns: to turn to the philosophy of science. After all, many philosophers of science have held that a distinctive feature of scientific inquiry is that it aims at objectivity, and that we should assess and criticise putatively 'scientific' practices in terms of whether or not they are objective. Unfortunately, the concept of objectivity is not straightforward. For example, in an influential article questioning the objectivity of the medical sciences, Stegenga defines an objective process as being 'not sensitive to researchers' personal idiosyncrasies and biases' (Stegenga, 2011, 499). This definition sounds plausible; it seems fairly clear that processes which are affected by biases are not objective. But, on reflection, it raises a series of questions: couldn't biases sometimes lead us to true claims? Don't we value the insights of idiosyncratic geniuses? Would our processes be any better at knowledge production if they were affected by shared, rather than idiosyncratic, biases? Can any process be entirely insensitive to researchers' idiosyncrasies?

In turn, these epistemological problems intersect with broader debates. On the one hand, they relate to metaphysical debates over realism and representation: in what sense is a quality like the efficacy of drugs 'out there', waiting to be discovered, and to what extent does it depend on us? On the other hand, they relate to debates over the proper relationship between science, society, politics and economics: can medical science ever be objective when so much is funded by the pharmaceutical industry? Would we be better-off were medical science nationalised?

We have no shortage of reasons, both practical and theoretical, to understand debates over the nature of scientific objectivity. The aim of this Element is to provide an overview of some of them. Of course, objectivity is a vast topic for a short study; as such, my coverage is partial. Specifically, I focus on four topics: the turn to trust in recent work on objectivity (Section 1); the relationship between biases, values and objectivity (Section 2); the relationship between objectivity and social structures (Section 3); and the relationship between objectivity and the notion of epistemic perspectives or situated knowledges (Section 4). Inevitably, I do not discuss these topics in as much depth as I would like, and there are many topics I would like to discuss but which I do not touch on at all; I warn the reader of any major gaps as I go along. The topic of objectivity is not only vast, but also controversial. I have tried to provide a balanced account of various debates, but I see no point in hiding my own opinion on some key debates. I do, however, try to warn the reader where I insert myself into the text. As we will see in Section 2, though, it is an interesting question whether being open about my own biases is enough for my claims to be objective!

1.1 Proliferating Senses of Objectivity

We can identify three constraints on any plausible account of scientific objectivity; it should be concerned with *representation*, pick out something *valuable* and it should be *viable*. Before going on, I shall explain these desiderata.

First, I take it that any account of objectivity should have some *fidelity* with our everyday uses of the term. In turn, I suggest that this implies that objectivity talk is primarily concerned with *practices of representation*. Although we use the term objective in a variety of ways – to refer to certain sorts of factual claims, or to certain processes for generating factual claims or to virtues of individual scientists – these uses are united by a sense that objectivity is concerned with representing the world; we care that evidence amalgamation methods in medicine are objective because, if they are not, we doubt that they will be accurate guides to figuring out whether drugs will work or not; we care that journalists are objective because they are supposed to tell us what is actually happening. Of course, in some cases, objectivity may be tied-up with virtues other than representational accuracy; for example, you might think it is important that a judge is 'objective' in the sense that she is impartial; or we might think it is important that scientists building a climate model are 'object-ive', even if the sense in which a model 'represents' the world is complex. Still, I suggest that, even in these trickier cases, talk of objectivity is often bound up with concerns about representation: the judge should be impartial because partiality gets in the way of reaching what, according to the law, would be the 'right' answer; a good climate model need not be accurate in every regard, but its goodness is, at least in part, a function of the accuracy of its predictions. By contrast, talk of objectivity seems a little strange in cases where there is no link to practices of representation. For example, it would seem odd to say that an engineer redesigning a toaster should be 'objective' in her work (although, tellingly, it does make sense to say that she should be objective in *reporting* the results of her work – say, whether the toaster really uses less electricity). Below, I will return to the obvious worry that notions of accurate representation are metaphysically tricky; still, that worry is separate from whether we think of scientific objectivity in terms of accurate representation.

In this sense, *scientific* objectivity needs to be distinguished from a different 'purely procedural' sense of objectivity, as following any old rule blindly. For example, imagine an examiner who blindly follows the exam marking guide-lines, placing her own sense of candidates' ability to one side. We might say that she acts objectively, even if we share her suspicion that those guidelines are fatally flawed as a guide to candidates' ability. When we talk about scientific processes as objective, though, we typically imply something more: that these processes help us represent the world well, rather than that they can be followed in a robotic manner. (Much more on this distinction to follow.)

Second, objectivity is epistemically *valuable*; we have good reason to ensure epistemic practices *are* objective and to trust objective practices. Of course, that is not to say that objectivity is always valuable; perhaps there are cases where we should bend the truth for the sake of some greater good. Nor is it to deny that there are important criticisms of objectivity, for example from feminist critics (see Section 4). Still, in general, it seems that we value objectivity, and any decent account of the concept should capture this thought.

Third, the concept of objectivity is supposed to be action-guiding, in the sense that it provides a yardstick for assessing and changing epistemic practices. As such, objectivity must be *viable*; even if it is impossible for a person, process or claim to be fully objective, it must be possible to be more or less objective. A nice question, to which we will return shortly, is how to relate this third desideratum to the first: the stronger our account of what is required for an 'objective' representation of the world, the harder it is to see how the notion of objectivity could guide action.

Beyond these three desiderata, matters get more complex. Megill (1994) thinks that there are four key senses of objectivity; Gaukroger lists five senses (Gaukroger, 2012, chapter 1); Douglas (2004) may seem more modest, suggesting three 'modes' of objectivity (in terms of processes of interaction with the world, features of individuals' thought processes and social procedures), but then suggests that each mode is further sub-divided into different forms. Most terrifyingly of all, in an influential article, Marianne Janack lists 13 senses of objectivity she has found in the literature:

(1) objectivity as value neutrality;

(2) objectivity as lack of bias, with bias understood as including: (a) personal attachment; (b) political aims; (c) ideological commitments; (d) preferences; (e) desires; (f) interests; (g) emotion;

(3) objectivity as scientific method;

(4) objectivity as rationality;

(5) objectivity as an attitude of 'psychological distance';

(6) objectivity as 'world-directedness';

(7) objectivity as impersonality;

(8) objectivity as impartiality;

(9) objectivity as having to do with facts;

(10) objectivity as having to do with things as they are in themselves; objectivity as universality;

(11) objectivity as disinterestedness;

(12) objectivity as commensurability;

(13) objectivity as intersubjective agreement (Janack, 2002, 275).

In short, everyone agrees that the term objectivity is used in a lot of ways (even if they disagree over how many).

Of course, it is possible that a term is used in various ways, but with a shared core meaning. For example, looking at Janack's list, we might think that the concept of objectivity as lack of bias (sense 2) stems from a concern that bias gets in the way of creating 'intersubjective agreement' (sense 13); that 'impersonality' (sense 7) is important for much the same reason; and so on. However, there are reasons to think that objectivity talk might not just be complex, but, in Douglas' phrase, 'irreducibly complex': that there may be no guarantee that all of the different senses of objectivity will coincide (Douglas, 2004).

Broadly, these reasons stem from the fact that contemporary notions of objectivity have a complex history. As Loraine Daston and Peter Galison

(2007) suggested in their monumental historical study, our understanding of the epistemic virtues that should guide practices of representation has shifted over time. Botanical illustrators or map-makers of the eighteenth century were guided by an ideal of 'truth to nature', according to which representations should capture the ideal type of a specimen, through removing blemishes and quirks. In the nineteenth century, however, the advent of technologies such as photography motivated a shift towards 'mechanical objectivity', in which scientists were expected to show restraint and let nature 'speak for itself'. In turn, in the twentieth century, this ideal gave way to a notion of the expert as exercising a kind of 'trained judgement', which allowed her to see the underlying patterns in data. These differing concepts do not neatly replace one another as we progress towards the one true view. Rather, they co-exist and jostle in shaping our sense of good representation, and, hence, what counts as objective. Of course, Daston and Galison's story is contestable, but the moral is simple enough: the concept of objectivity has a complex history, and, as Nietzsche claimed, 'only that which has no history can be defined'.

1.2 Processes and Products

Despite these complexities, it seems possible to distinguish two main approaches to understanding objectivity: first, as a feature of certain kinds of epistemic products; second, as a feature of certain kinds of epistemic processes (Reiss and Sprenger, 2017). I will explore these two approaches and their relationship, and sketch why, over the last few decades, philosophers of science have increasingly focused on the second.

On the first approach, some epistemic product – say, a factual belief or claim – is 'objective' or 'objectively true' if it represents some feature of the world as it really is, rather than as it appears to us; in Koskinen's nice formulation, it is knowledge of 'the object untainted by the distortions caused by our subjectivity' (Koskinen, 2018, 3). To motivate this general worry, consider the concern that claims such as 'grass is green' are not fully objective, because 'greenness' is a 'secondary quality', that is one which depends, in some sense, on human observers (Menzies and Price, 1993). The view of objectivity as somehow related to representing reality apart from humans is appealing, but horribly hard to pin down. As such, it is often expressed in metaphorical language: for example, in Thomas Nagel's metaphor of objectivity in terms of a 'view from nowhere', achieved through detachment from 'the contingencies of the self' (Nagel, 1986) or in Bernard Williams' concept of the 'absolute conception' of the world (Williams, 1985).

There are multiple versions of the second 'process' account of objectivity. However, they typically all have at their core a sense of objective processes as more or less rule-governed activities, relatively immune to features of the individuals who undertake them; for example, consider Stegenga's characterisation of objectivity in medical science as insensitivity to personal or idiosyncratic biases. On such views, objectivity is primarily a feature of the ways in which we investigate the world, rather than the products of our investigations. Note that, on the process view, the product of some investigation need not count as part of the furniture of the Universe to count as objective. For example, claims about drug effectiveness might not appear in the basic ontological inventory, but be 'objective' as long as they result from certain sorts of processes which minimise bias.[1]

Distinguishing these two senses of objectivity is central to many philosophical disputes. Consider a non-scientific example: some philosophers worry that moral claims – for example, that murder is wrong – are not objective. Often, such claims involve an (implicit or explicit) juxtaposition with scientific claims. Worries about moral objectivity are often motivated by the (alleged) fact of widespread moral disagreement (Mackie, 1977). Broadly, however, we can distinguish two kinds of moral anti-realist worry. One is that moral claims are not objective in the sense that there are no moral facts to which they can correspond (consider the argument for moral scepticism along the lines that 'were there moral facts, disagreement would not be so widespread'). The second is that moral claims are not objective in the sense that there is no widely shared criterion for resolving moral disagreement (consider the argument for moral scepticism that 'were there a widely shared criterion, disagreement would be more easily resolved'). We might respond to the second of these worries – show that there is some criterion which we do, or should, all use to solve moral disputes – without responding to the first – that is without showing that moral properties are out there in nature. For some, establishing such a criterion would suffice for moral objectivity, whereas for others, a worry would remain.

We see similar worries in philosophy of science. Consider a striking example from twentieth century philosophy of science. Thomas Kuhn's *Structure of Scientific Revolutions* argued for an understanding of science as involving two stages (Kuhn, 1962). During normal science, scientists are engaged in 'problem solving' within some paradigm, a shared set of rules, principles and exemplars; during periods of revolution, a paradigm gives way to a second paradigm,

---

[1] There are multiple ways of distinguishing these two forms of objectivity; for example, see Axtell's pragmatist distinction between 'ontological' *versus* 'cognitive' senses of objectivity (Axtell, 2015, 2–4)

radically changing the problems that scientists work on, how they work on them and what counts as success. Kuhn's work is often claimed to have challenged beliefs about the objectivity of science.[2] However, in these discussions, we often find two distinct issues run together. One set of concerns is that Kuhn's claims about the role of paradigms in shaping scientific practice implies that we always make claims about the world from *within* a particular position. Specifically, Kuhn seems to suggest that, because all scientific research is paradigm-bound, it is extremely difficult to compare paradigms as better-or-worse; what counts as a key problem and as a way of resolving a problem in *my* paradigm may differ fundamentally from what counts as a key problem or successful solution in *your* paradigm. If so, it seems that there is no way of comparing paradigms in terms of which one is closer to the world as it 'really' is. Kuhn's work seems, then, to threaten the objectivity of scientific products (or strictly, our ability to know whether our products are objectively true or not).

A second set of concerns, however, focuses on Kuhn's account of paradigm change. Famously, Kuhn (apparently) suggested that there was no general pattern or logic to paradigm changes, but, rather, that shifts occurred as the result of contingent sociological factors, suggesting a version of what is sometimes called Planck's principle, that 'a new scientific truth does not triumph by convincing its opponents and making them see the light, but rather because its opponents eventually die and a new generation grows up that is familiar with it' (Planck, 1950, 33). As Kuhn himself later acknowledged, in his seminal work he seemed to suggest that the *process* of theory change is not objective, but a matter of mob psychology (Kuhn, 1977).

Of course, Kuhn's claims about how paradigms structure science and about how paradigms change are linked. However, they can be distinguished, with important implications for how we think about objectivity. For example, in later work, Kuhn (1977) presented an account of change based around the idea that scientists choose between paradigms on the basis of their possession of certain sorts of epistemic virtues. Unfortunately, he suggested, given that there are a plurality of epistemic virtues, and no obvious way in which to rank them, different scientists might come to different epistemic judgements about which paradigm to prefer. However, despite these problems, he suggested that the process of paradigm change could be 'objective', as the community could provide judgements about which virtues to favour, and, hence, which paradigms to adopt, that were not swayed by individual investigators' preferences. We might concede that Kuhn's later theory does show that scientific change can be

---

[2] For a short but stimulating account of how Kuhn's work relates to broadly Kantian notions of objectivity, see Gaukroger, 2012, chapter 5

'objective', in the sense that it is not affected by idiosyncrasies and biases, related, perhaps, to Daston and Galison's notion of trained judgement. However, even granting this, we might still be worried that Kuhn's work challenges the objectivity of science, insofar as it implies that our paradigms always structure our experience, such that we can never step back and ask which scientific theory represents the world as it really is.

As the example of Kuhn's shifting views suggests, it is *possible* to provide an account of objective scientific processes that does not necessarily respond to concerns about the objectivity of scientific products. Still, you might think that when we are talking about scientific objectivity, the product sense is more important than the process sense; that the ultimate aim of science is to help us somehow pull back the filters we impose to show us the world as it really is. From this perspective, Kuhn missed something in his response to his critics: the important worry about his work is that theory change might not get us closer to a true picture, rather than that it is affected by idiosyncrasies. However, although the conception of objectivity in terms of revealing the fundamental structure of the world may still be popular in some circles, it does not seem central to recent philosophy of science.[3]

An enjoyable article by Elisabeth Lloyd (1995) provides a neat summary of many of the concerns about the notion that science is – or ought to be – in the game of achieving the 'view from nowhere.' For Lloyd, what she calls talk of the 'really Real' or 'big O' objectivity is a 'philosophical folk story' (Lloyd, 1994, 353), which fails on multiple grounds. It is premised on an implausible reductionist metaphysics, of the world as arranged in hierarchical layers wrapped up with a discredited religious worldview; even if this metaphysical view is correct, it may be impossible for us, limited human creatures, to see the world as it really is; even if we could achieve the view from nowhere, it would be impossible for us to know that we had. Using the terminology above, Lloyd suggests that the notion of objectivity as the 'really Real' is not *viable*. To add to Lloyd's attack, we might note that even if we can achieve 'big O' objectivity, it is not clear that this conception has fidelity with our everyday uses of the term. For example, no-one thinks that the current UK inflation rate is part of the metaphysical furniture of the Universe. If anything depends on human perceptions, interactions and evaluative practices, then 'inflation' does. Nonetheless, we can and do talk of more or less objective ways of constructing inflation indices or measuring inflation or reporting changes to inflation. In short, even if

---

[3] It is worth being careful here: outside philosophy of science, there is still a tendency to think that *true* objectivity involves something like talking about what is really there, rather than merely having certain sorts of non-biased processes. Quite why this should be the case is interesting, but not my concern here.

the absolute conception were *viable*, it is not clear that it captures our everyday sense that a wide range of things – not just the basic things – can be represented more or less objectively.

It is now far more common for philosophers of science to conceive of objectivity primarily in terms of a feature of processes. One important driver of this shift is the kinds of metaphysical and epistemological concerns expressed by Lloyd.[4] A second important driver is the link that many philosophers draw between objectivity and trust. Following a suggestion made by Arthur Fine (1998) in an attack on the Nagel/Williams picture, many philosophers stress the pragmatic functions of objectivity talk as a way of signalling epistemic trustworthy sources of information.[5] Specifically, Fine's key intervention has two moves: first, he dismisses the notion that we can have any way of getting to the 'really Real' on a wide variety of grounds; second, he suggests that we can best understand objectivity talk in terms of its function, as helping us identify which kinds of scientific process are useful to us. Ultimately, then, he suggests that objectivity is simply 'that in the process of inquiry which makes for trust in the outcome of inquiry'.

It is easy to see how a focus on trust can lead us to a focus on process, by thinking about the problems non-experts face in assessing expert testimony (Goldman, 2001). Imagine that you must decide whether or not to trust some informant. Typically, we turn to informants precisely when we ourselves cannot distinguish true from false claims in some domain; if we knew what was true, we wouldn't need informants! Simply saying that some informant's epistemic product is 'objectively' true does not give us any further reason to believe that informant; it is a bit like responding to 'why should I believe what you just said?' by answering 'because it is really, really true'. By contrast, saying that the product was arrived at by an 'objective' process does give us some reason to accept the informant's claim: we can check whether she really followed that process, we can check whether we think that process really is objective; and so on. Thinking about objectivity as a feature of processes seems to help us in our everyday task of placing and withholding trust, in a way in which thinking about it as a feature of products does not. For practical purposes, then, there are excellent reasons to focus on objectivity of process, rather than product.

---

[4] In the name of fairness, as Lloyd herself notes, it is unclear whether even apparent defenders of 'big O' objectivity were ever really committed to very strong metaphysical and epistemological claims

[5] Although Fine's suggestion that we focus on the link between objectivity and trustworthiness can be detached from any particular metaphysical views about the 'view from nowhere', Fine also had a horse in that race, suggesting that many metaphysical disputes about realism rest on a kind of mistake; see, for example Fine, 1984

The claim that objectivity is bound up with notions of trust provides us, then, with reasons to focus on the objectivity of processes, rather than products. Before moving on, it is worth quickly noting an important ambiguity in the literature on objectivity and trust. Very broadly, we can distinguish two senses of 'trust': first, a rich, thick sense where 'trust' is bound up with broadly ethical concerns and face-to-face relationships; second, a thin sense, where 'trust' means something more like 'a willingness to rely'. This distinction has been central in broader philosophical debates about the nature of trust (Hawley, 2014). Which sense is relevant to thinking about objectivity? Consider some examples: a scientist writing a paper who must decide whether to use reports from co-authors scattered across the globe (Kukla, 2012); a non-scientist watching a documentary who must decide whether to accept the experts' claims that climate change is serious (John, 2018). It seems natural to describe both of these cases as involving decisions to place epistemic trust, and as cases where a key question involves the objectivity of informants, but, in neither case does the relevant relationship seem to involve deep, thick ethical assumptions and commitments. Therefore, I suggest that, in thinking about trust and objectivity in science, it is more sensible to interpret trust in the second, thinner sense. Indeed, similar concerns have led Inkeri Koskinen (2018) to suggest that, in analysing scientific objectivity, we should replace 'trust' talk with 'reliance'. Koskinen has an important point. However, as Daston and Galison point out, historically, notions of objectivity have been caught up with notions of virtue. Regardless of whether we *ought* to think of scientific objectivity as having an ethical component, we often *do* think that way. Using the language of trust helps remind us of these important complexities and ambiguities.

With this caveat in place, which processes count as objective, though? Heather Douglas (2004) has distinguished three kinds of processes – processes of engagement with the world, individual thought processes and social processes that produce results – each of which can be characterised in terms of being more or less objective along various dimensions. For example, she suggests that one use of 'objective' is to describe processes of engagement with the world that involve 'manipulation' of objects ('manipulable' objectivity), where manipulability may come in degrees; another sense is to describe social processes that allow for strong interaction and contestation between scientists ('interactive objectivity'), which, again, can come in degrees; and so on. Perhaps *the* key question in the recent literature is whether there is some common epistemic thread running through the different senses of objectivity beyond a link to trust? Douglas suspects not: that objectivity is an irredeemably complex concept. Others disagree; for example, Koskinen (2018) argues that all senses of objectivity are united in that they are concerned with strategies for the minimisation of what she calls 'epistemic risk'. On this account, the complexity of objectivity talk arises because different kinds of 'epistemic risk' are relevant in different sciences (for more on this view, see Section 4).

1.3 Against Purely Procedural Objectivity

In the next two sections, then, I will look at some attempts to characterise the objectivity of processes. Before doing so, however, it is worth noting an ambiguity in the notion of process. As I noted above, we sometimes talk of objectivity to mean something like 'following the rules, whatever they are, irrespective of one's own inclinations'. It is important to distinguish this thin, purely procedural, sense of objectivity from a concern with the objectivity of processes in the sense that grounds epistemic trust. Consider, again, Kuhn's work. Imagine that Kuhn had argued that scientists choose paradigms on the basis of coin-tosses. We can imagine that a scientist might follow this process in an entirely 'procedurally objective' manner – she tosses the coin and chooses paradigms accordingly, regardless of her own views and inclinations ('what a shame it was heads! Tails looked far better to me'). Still, it is hard to imagine anyone arguing that the process of coin-tossing is a *good* process for deciding which paradigms to adopt; certainly, it is hard to see why this process would ground epistemic trust in science. By contrast, we can tell some story about how and why scientists' collective judgements about the epistemic merits of different theories *might* ground trust in those theories. In what follows, I assume, then, that an account of objectivity should focus on *process*, rather than merely *procedural*, objectivity. That is to say, it should tell us why a process, if followed correctly, generates epistemically trustworthy products, rather than merely that the process can be followed in a robotic or algorithmic way. By 'epistemically trustworthy products', I mean products which we have good reason to believe are – or are likely to be – accurate representations of the world.

Before going on, two clarifications. First, the concept of representation is not intended to be metaphysically demanding. Plausibly, we can have more or less accurate estimates of whether or not some drug is effective regardless of whether drug effectiveness is part of the furniture of the Universe. There are tricky metaphysical issues here, but the notion of accurate representation is not simply a way to sneak 'big O objectivity' in through the back door. Rather, all that is required is what Janack calls a 'common-sense realism' (Janack, 2002, 268). Second, you might worry that the language of representation is a bad way to think about some scientific products, but that we can still think of the processes leading to those products as being objective. Most obviously, there are well-known problems with thinking about scientific models straightforwardly as representations of the world (Bolinska, 2013). Nonetheless, we might still think that a process for developing a model can be more or less objective; for example, we might be more willing to trust a model of disease progression produced by independent scientists than one developed by industry-funded researchers. Again, there are tricky issues here, but, for current purposes, they can be bracketed; we can start with an account of objectivity in processes which clearly aim at representing the world, and then extend our account to more complex cases, such as models, which may involve concerns with partial representation.

Beyond philosophical housekeeping, stressing the distinction between procedural and process objectivity is important because the two can be conflated, with potentially bad effects. To see why, note that if we are concerned with purely procedural objectivity, then, typically, we will prefer processes in terms of how easy it is to follow them in a simple, algorithmic fashion, or how easy it is to check that they have been followed algorithmically. For example, if *all* we cared about was that rules for theory choice could be followed in a purely procedural manner, then we would prefer a process of coin-tossing over a process of communal weighing-up of various epistemic desiderata. This is despite the fact that the latter method might seem a far better way of grounding trust. That is a silly example, intended purely for exposition. Note, however, that in some circumstances, we might value purely procedural objectivity for broadly non-epistemic reasons, regardless of its epistemic merits; if there is a clear rule, it is easy to check whether people have cheated, to predict how people will draw inferences and so on. As such, there might be a tension between two desiderata: ensuring that our processes are (or can be seen to be) 'procedurally objective' and ensuring 'process objectivity' – that is, that our processes generate accurate representations.

This is a subtle distinction. To make it concrete, consider Theodore Porter's influential historical account of the growth of quantification in science (Porter, 1994). Today, we often think of quantification as a kind of mark or sign of scientificity – some epistemic activity is only a proper, 'objective' science if it has numbers involved.[6] However, Porter suggests that, historically, the drive to quantification has as much to do with a bureaucratic need to have simple, transparent systems as a wish to represent accurately. Indeed, Porter suggests that there is a general pattern whereby in a public measurement system, such as those employed by state bureaucracies, standardisation (that like cases be – and/or

---

[6] It is worth noting that Porter frames his historical narrative in terms where 'numbers' come to replace 'trust'. That might seem in tension with the claims above that objectivity, which we now often associate with the numerical, is bound up with trust. However, what is really happening here is that Porter thinks of trust in what I called the 'rich' sense above. In the terminology above, Porter's concern is that this rich trust becomes impossible in the modern scientific world, and is replaced with mere reliance

be seen to be – treated alike) and proper surveillance are important values. These values give rise to a 'strong incentive to prefer readily standardizable measures to highly accurate ones' (Porter, 1994, 391). He proposes, for example, that were one manufacturer to use 'state-of-the-art' analysis to assess toxicity, this would be 'viewed as a vexing source of interlaboratory bias, and very likely an effort to get more favorable measures by evading the usual protocol, not as a welcome improvement in accuracy' (Porter, 1994, 391)! Porter's fascinating story suggests that we should be careful; clearly, even if being easy to follow is a political or social virtue, it is not obviously an epistemic virtue.[7]

If all we mean by scientific objectivity is something like 'standardised' or 'rule-based', then a huge number of processes for generating epistemic products, coin-tossing, say, can be objective. As Porter points out, this kind of objectivity may be extremely valuable for all sorts of non-epistemic reasons. However, being objective in this sense does not provide us with any particular epistemic reasons to trust the products which those processes generate. To characterise scientific objectivity, then, we need an account of how and when epistemic processes generate epistemically trustworthy products. It would certainly be *nice* if those processes were also relatively straightforward, relatively easy to check-up on, hard to cheat and so on – but these are not the same as the processes *themselves* being objective.

2 Values, Interests and Ideals

Given its complex history, its contested role in social and political debate, and its link to controversial topics across philosophy, how in the world can we go about saying what makes epistemic processes 'objective'? Consider a suggestion made by Amartya Sen (2009) about the concept of justice. Justice, like objectivity, is a highly contested and complex notion. However, Sen notes, there is often a high degree of agreement on what counts as an injustice. For example, even if we disagree over whether or not a perfectly just society would be colour-blind, we might agree that contemporary racist institutions are unjust. Studying injustice might then be practically and theoretically more fruitful than trying to analyse justice directly. Similar considerations seem pertinent to the case of objectivity. As we saw above, there are many different ways of characterising what objectivity is; so, why not start by asking, instead, what it is not? Rather than identify features of processes that make them objective, we should, instead, study factors that make them non-objective.

---

[7] For an attempt to turn Porter's historical account into a philosophical theory of how an epistemically empty number can play an important social and political role, see Badano, John and Junghans, 2017

There are particularly good reasons to adopt Sen's general strategy in our specific case. Ian Hacking (2015) states that objectivity is an empty concept because it is essentially negative, in the sense that to say a procedure is objective is to say that it is *not* affected in some way – say, by a researcher's biases – rather than to cite some positive feature of the process. I return to Hacking's scepticism in Section 4; for now, though, we can accept that there is some truth in his claim that, typically, objectivity is a matter of absence, rather than presence. So, in this section, I focus on distortions and impediments to objectivity.

Specifically, in the literature, we find that three kinds of influences on scientific processes are often treated as impediments to objectivity: biases, interests and ethical/political values. To give some examples, consider three cases: a scientist who implicitly believes that black people are inferior to white people and interprets her data in ways that exaggerate certain sorts of differences between these groups (a case of bias); a scientist who is resistant to evidence that some product is unsafe because she has a financial stake in the success of that product (a case of interest); or a scientist who steadfastly refuses to engage with a data set showing that GM crops are safe because she has a strong commitment to maintaining unspoiled nature (a case of non-epistemic values). In all three cases, it seems fairly clear that, by letting their biases, interests or values influence their reasoning, these scientists have somehow failed to be fully objective. It also seems obvious that processes which guard against these kinds of influences would be more objective. What, though, unites these various factors? And, just as importantly, which factors might influence scientific reasoning without undermining its objectivity?

In this section, then, I will do three things: first, I will outline what I take to be one simple and appealing way of spelling out the notion of distorting influences, in terms of 'wants' that involve a deviation from epistemic rationality. I then outline how this 'simple account of process objectivity' relates to the distinction between individual and social notions of objectivity. Finally, I consider one of the most powerful objections to the simple view: the argument from inductive risk, which implies that at least one class of 'distortions' – non-epistemic value commitments – cannot and should not be completely isolated from scientific reasoning. I conclude by considering two responses to this objection, from Torsten Wilholt and from Gregor Betz.

2.1 Introducing the Simple View of Process Objectivity: Against Wanting

There is a rather obvious way of spelling out why biases, interests and values might seem problematic. There are some commonly shared norms of epistemic rationality, relevant to the task of representing the world accurately; for example, that our beliefs ought to be guided by the available evidence. Biases, interests and non-epistemic values might influence research in ways that lead to deviations from epistemic rationality; for example, by leading us to overlook or downplay certain sorts of evidence. Therefore, there are clear reasons why, in general, we might be suspicious of research that is influenced by these factors. However, these remarks are rather empty. After all, there are very many influences on research that might hamper our ability to represent the world accurately, but not all of these influences necessarily undermine objectivity. A lack of money might mean that we are unable to invest in the best equipment for some investigation, but we would not necessarily say that a wealthier research team is thereby more objective than a poorer research team. I suggest what links biases, interests and non-epistemic values as impediments to the *objectivity* of research is that they seem to involve the intrusion of *wants* or *desires* into the pursuit of science.

To explain, it seems clear that there is often a difference between the way the world *is* and the way in which we *want* the world to be (or the way we want to *say* the world is). For example, I may want the world to be free of hunger, but that is different from the world being free of hunger; in writing a promotion application, I may want to say that my work is highly influential, but, unfortunately, this does not mean that my work *is* highly influential. What unites biases, non-epistemic interests and non-epistemic values, and distinguishes them from other impediments, is that they are all influences that risk leading us to conclusions which (in a very broad sense) we *want* to be true, rather than which are true. This is most obvious when we think about the concept of 'interests': the fact I have a financial interest in the success of a drug means that I want the study to show that the drug is safe; this influence can, then, interfere with my ability to judge whether the drug is safe. Something similar is true about the influence of values on research (albeit in a slightly more complex way): because I want to be able to *say* that the world is just, I close myself off from evidence that would render my claim insincere.[8] Finally, consider biases; for example, the so-called 'confirmation bias', that we tend to weigh evidence which *confirms* our antecedent beliefs more heavily than evidence which *contradicts* them. We can think of such cases as ones where a wish to preserve a kind of cognitive economy leads us to 'want' the evidence to be a certain way, distorting our grasp of what the evidence actually implies.

---

[8] As these examples suggest, I think that we should distinguish the psychological mechanism of 'wishful thinking' – where our wants that the world is some way sub-consciously influence our beliefs – and 'wishful speaking' – where our wants to be able to say that some claim is established influence our attempts to prove that claim. Both processes might undermine objectivity, but they are, otherwise, very different (John, 2019)

(Before going on, a clarification: some authors are very careful to distinguish between, say, biases and interests; others sometimes lump them together, using 'bias' or 'non-epistemic values' to refer to *any* of these three kinds of influence. I think it is important to distinguish the general phenomenon of 'want-based influences' from particular kinds of influences – but an overview is not the best place for legislating others' usage. I suggest to the reader that she is very careful when she gets to the literature to be aware that one writer's 'interests' may be another writer's 'non-epistemic values'.)

At this point, we face an obvious question: as I have acknowledged, there are very many factors that might influence our ability to represent the world – say, lack of time or the sheer difficulty of inference. Why, then, have a concept of objectivity, which seems to pick out a particular class of influences – 'want-based commitments' – as somehow particularly problematic? To be frank, I am not certain. I suspect there is some complex link between objectivity and moral notions of deceit and trickery; it is somehow ethically worse to get to false claims through a non-objective process than, say, because you ran out of money. Unfortunately, that is a conjecture, not an argument. All I want to stress here is that objectivity language does not cover *all* of the ways in which investigations might fall short, but a particularly important or salient sub-class: where wants or desires have dislodged epistemic norms.

Note that want-based influences on procedures are not *bound* to lead us to form false beliefs. For example, it is entirely possible both that my reasoning is affected by a confirmation bias *and* that my current hypothesis is true, such that having the bias helps me retain a true belief. It is possible that I have an interest in the drug being safe, which leads me to overvalue certain sorts of evidence, *and* the drug is actually safe, such that overvaluing that evidence was epistemically helpful. Indeed, some argue that various heuristics and biases that affect human reasoning can be viewed as a kind of evolutionary adaptation, which have developed because, in most cases, they are a cognitively cheap 'good enough' shortcut (Gigerenzer and Selten, 2002). Nonetheless, it seems plausible that reasoning which is guided only by norms of epistemic rationality is preferable to reasoning which is affected by want-based influences. For example, it seems plausible that medical research has improved as systematic observation has come to dislodge reasoning which was subject to various cognitive biases (Bird, 2019). Scientific reasoning processes which are not influenced by wantings are *more likely* to generate true representations, and, as such, are more trustworthy. I will call this general picture the 'simple account of process objectivity'.

One nice feature of this general picture is that it allows us to justify a popular distinction between 'epistemic' or 'cognitive' and 'non-epistemic' or 'non-cognitive' values (McMullin, 1982). Once we move away from highly simpli-fied toy examples, actual scientific practice is shot through with considerations which are not simply about the evidence to hand. For example, famously, scientists often appeal to the fact that some theory is simpler than a second as a reason to prefer that theory. On the face of it, such reasoning is questionable; there is no obvious reason why nature should be simple rather than complex. Nonetheless, we might try to justify the place of considerations such as simpli-city in scientific reasoning by showing that these considerations are, in the long run, truth-tropic. For example, it is easier to test simple rather than complex theories; therefore, if scientists start by testing a simple theory they are likely to get to the actually correct theory more quickly than if they start with testing the more complex theory (Douglas, 2009, chapter 5). By contrast, there is no obvious long-term *epistemic* rationale for a general preference for, say, theories that promote social justice; this epistemic strategy reflects a desire about how the world ought to be, rather than a strategy for figuring out how the world is. Hence, while appeals to 'theoretical simplicity' and appeals to 'fits with social justice' both seem to go *beyond* the evidence, the former can apparently be justified in epistemic terms in a way in that the latter cannot.[9]

2.2 Clarifying the Simple View of Process Objectivity: Justification, Not Discovery

The simple account of process objectivity seems important in many invocations of objectivity. When the Chinese Ministry of Foreign Affairs accuses journalists of a lack of objectivity, that claim is intended to suggest that they allow their political agendas to get in the way of providing an accurate account of the world. Or consider, again, the fuss caused by Kuhn's work, with its (apparent) sugges-tion that scientists chose paradigms in order to win certain sorts of social prestige, rather than because of their epistemic qualities. Clearly, if anything seems like a want-based distortion of good epistemic reasoning, it is the politicking of trying to get ahead in academia. As another telling example, consider Bertolaso and Sterpetti's claim that, in cancer research 'conclusions do diverge. This means that prior probabilities are not objectively assigned, i.e. they are not assigned by means of a (potentially mechanisable) procedure which can univocally determine each prior in an uncontroversial way' (Bertolaso and Sterpetti, 2019, 3300).

However, the account also requires some tweaking in response to various concerns. First, there are various ways in which non-epistemic values, biases

---

[9] For an extremely helpful discussion of various related issues, and their links to the later parts of this section, see Steel, 2010

and interests do and should structure the pursuit of science, which seem entirely compatible with science being objective and trustworthy. This is most obvious in the case of non-epistemic values, which clearly structure how scientists research, as, for example, when concerns about individual autonomy demand that researchers gain participants' informed consent. Non-epistemic values also play an important role in affecting what scientists research, as, for example, when funding bodies prioritise research on the basis of what will have greater social value. Although we might sometimes think that these non-epistemic influences are in tension with various epistemic goals, it does not follow that the results scientists obtain are, thereby, epistemically problematic. For example, I might think that government science policy is problematic in the sense that we would gain more epistemic benefit were scientists to research the causes of the Big Bang rather than the causes of cancer, but it does not follow that I think that research on the causes of cancer is inherently non-objective or untrustworthy. It seems wrong to say that *all* cases where non-epistemic commitments structure scientific research, are non-objective. This is just as well, because many of those constraints – for example, limitations on animal and human experimentation – seem entirely reasonable.

It seems, then, that we need to specify the ways in which non-epistemic values (biases, interests, etc.) influence research more carefully to characterise what counts as objective. One obvious option is to say that these influences are problematic when they involve some commitment to arriving at a particular result (as opposed to researching a particular topic, or using particular methods). For example, we might think it is permissible for scientists to research cancer because they have a strong non-epistemic commitment to curing cancer, but problematic for them to study this topic with the sole intent of showing the efficacy of a particular treatment in which they have a financial interest. Indeed, it is worth noting that, very often, such concerns are thrown around in everyday debate employing the language of objectivity. For example, climate sceptics sometimes object that climate scientists cannot be trusted, because they already have a strong commitment, linked to their left-wing agendas to show that climate change is real. (And, of course, conversely, climate scientists often claim that climate sceptics are untrustworthy because their non-epistemic commitments colour their judgement.)

However, there are worries about assuming that *interested* research is necessarily untrustworthy. At least sometimes, scientists' non-epistemic commitments to a particular claim can be epistemically productive. As an example, consider Elizabeth Anderson's fascinating case-study of how a group of sociologists, explicitly motivated by feminist aims, upended the standard story about the long-term effects of divorce on children (Anderson, 2004). These researchers were concerned that research 'showing' that divorce is bad for children's well-being was being used to maintain restrictions on divorce, hence restricting women's agency. Motivated by these concerns, they undertook a series of studies which showed that, even if divorce has significant short-term effects on children, the long-term effects are insignificant – children 'bounce back' well from the initial shock of divorce. In this case, it seems that an explicitly acknowledged desire to achieve a non-epistemic end *promoted*, rather than *impeded*, the production of trustworthy knowledge, by shifting attention from the short term to the long term. In turn, it is easy to see that lots of cases might have a similar structure; perhaps researchers' financial interests in promoting a drug can help them design an experiment that furthers our knowledge.

I suggest, then, that the best way of understanding the simple view of process objectivity is in terms of the old-fashioned distinction between scientific discovery and scientific justification. A defender of process objectivity should concede that want-based-influences can play an important, perhaps essential, role in prompting scientists to do science and make important discoveries. What she should also hold, however, is that those influences cannot or should not play any role when scientists seek to justify these claims as true. So, for example, we might say that, even if their commitments to feminist goals played an important role in leading Anderson's researchers to their findings, these commitments play no proper role in justifying *belief* in their conclusions. In justifying *why* we should believe that divorce has minimal long-term effects, researchers should appeal only to their evidence, not the fit between this belief and their political goals. (Before going on, it is important to note that contemporary philosophers of science are, for good reasons, very sceptical of drawing a strong distinction between discovery and justification. Nonetheless, there is clearly some difference between the processes by which we come to some claim and the reasons we give for believing that claim; when a scientific paper sets out the evidence in favour of some conclusion, it does not list all of the reasons why those data were collected in the first place (Schickore, 2008). This workday sense of discovery and justification is all that is needed here.)

These remarks help us better understand the relationship between the simple view of process objectivity and what is sometimes called the 'Value Free Ideal' for science. Consider a formulation of the latter from Gregor Betz: 'the justification of scientific findings should not be based on non-epistemic (e.g. political or moral) grounds' (Betz, 2013, 1). It seems fairly clear that Betz's statement is not intended to rule out non-epistemic influences on what we research, but only on what we count as justified. It is also closely related to a principle that Hugh Lacey calls 'impartiality', which claims that moral, social and other non-cognitive values play 'no (proper) role in judgments of acceptance' (Lacey, 2005, 232). (Strictly, Lacey thinks that the Value Free Ideal consists of three principles – impartiality, neutrality and autonomy, but he is suspicious of neutrality and autonomy). In turn, the Value Free Ideal seems to provide a way of taking the vague thought that certain factors *distort* objectivity and render it more precise: scientific objectivity is not necessarily compromised just because scientists have biases or interests or value-commitments. If it were, scientific objectivity would be impossible and worthless! Rather, it is compromised when those non-epistemic commitments influence the epistemic core of scientific reasoning.[10]

Unfortunately, even when suitably qualified, the simple view of process objectivity faces two challenges: first, *can* we isolate scientific reasoning from the influence of non-epistemic factors (and, even if so, should we)? Second, is there a neat dividing-line between the epistemic and the non-epistemic at all? I discuss the second challenge in Section 3. In the rest of this section, I focus on the first. Specifically, we can divide the first challenge into two worries. The first I call the 'empirical' worry: that it is impossible, as a matter of fact, for scientific reasoning to be 'unbiased', 'value free' or, more generally, separated from what we want. The second I call the 'in-principle' worry: that, given the nature of scientific reasoning, scientists *must* (in a logical or ethical) sense appeal to 'non-epistemic values' in justification.

2.3 The Empirical Challenge to the Simple View: the Move to the Social Perspective

The empirical worry is very straightforward. Science is done by humans. Humans are influenced by a wide range of cognitive biases and come to their work with antecedent sets of interests and values. It is difficult to see how these non-epistemic commitments can be overcome. Therefore, the simple account of objectivity must be flawed, on the grounds that it demands of humans something they simply cannot do: it is not *viable*. Fortunately for defenders of the simple view, there is an obvious, equally simple answer to this challenge: to move to a social, rather than individual, perspective.

So far, I have been very vague about whether we should think of objectivity as a feature of *individual thought processes* or as a feature of *social processes*.

---

[10] Before going on, it is worth noting that the Value Free Ideal is often linked to positivism. However, as Axtell points out, leading positivists such as Carnap seemed to leave many issues as to be settled by 'expedience', making their relationship to the Value Free Ideal rather murky (Axtell, 2015, 78). Indeed, there is an interesting historical question as to whether anyone ever held a full-blown version of the Value Free Ideal until it was named and shamed as the 'dominant' position in philosophy of science by its 'opponents'

However, this is an important distinction (both for understanding the empirical worry and much the rest of this Element). It is clear that distortions in *individual-level* reasoning can be corrected through *social processes*. To take a simple example, consider the case of cognitive biases, such as the availability heuristic, where, in everyday reasoning, we tend to overstate the epistemic relevance of the evidence which happens to be most recent and vividly to mind. Plausibly, it is very difficult for individual reasoners to overcome this bias (indeed, as noted above, it may even be evolutionarily advantageous for humans to be swayed by this bias). Nonetheless, it seems that it might be corrected by social processes; for example, that others might point out to us the ways in which we are incorrectly overgeneralising from our own experience (Peters, 2020). At a more structural level, there are various broadly economics-inspired models of the social reward structure in society, which aim to show how social institutions might incentivise self-interested researchers, motivated only by a concern for fame and glory, to work in ways that promote the epistemic common good (Kitcher, 1990).

Beyond the fact that thinking about social structures helps block some concerns about objectivity, there is a more principled reason for adopting this stance, related to the link between trust and objectivity. When we are asked to trust scientists, we are asked to trust what they *say* about the world, rather than what they privately believe about the world. The speech act of making claims is, in turn, more than a mere articulation of what you happen to believe, but structured and influenced by social norms and processes. Of course, you might hope that scientists' individual beliefs – the result of individual thought processes – line-up with what they say in public – the result of social processes – but it is not clear why this matters to the trustworthiness of their utterances (John, 2019). Therefore, the defender of the simple account of objectivity need not, and should not, be committed to the thought that scientists are, can be or should be reasoning automata. Rather, she should hold that objectivity is a feature of social processes that give rise to social products in the form of public claims about the world.

To give a more concrete sense of this social strategy, consider some debates between philosophers of science and historians and sociologists of science. Science is an activity done by interacting individuals. We have excellent reasons to think that these individuals are subject to all sorts of cognitive biases and heuristics, which might distort their reasoning in predictable ways. Nonetheless, sometimes, within these communities, a consensus viewpoint emerges. What is the status of that consensus? Historians and sociologists of science have often accused philosophers of a kind of blindness on this question: when they think that the consensus position is likely to be true, they tend to assume that it emerged through reasoned discussion and debate, governed solely by epistemic norms. When they think that the consensus position was wrong, they tend to explain its emergence by appeal to the vagaries of social psychology. However, this asymmetry between 'good' and 'bad' forms of consensus seems deeply implausible. Presumably, if biases, non-epistemic commitments and various kinds of social pressure are part of the history of 'bad' consensus formation, they are just as likely to be part of the history of 'good' consensus formation.

In an influential paper, Miriam Solomon (1994) provided a nice way of thinking about some of these knotty issues.[11] For Solomon, there is no need to make an empirically implausible claim that 'rational' consensus-formation processes are in place in 'good' cases and radically different 'irrational' consensus-formation processes are in place in 'bad' cases. Rather, she argues that we can, as it were, 'magic up' a good consensus; even heavily biased agents can end up agreeing on claims with a high degree of empirical success, depending on the details of their interaction with nature and with one another. What Solomon calls a 'normative consensus' – that is, a consensus which we ought to trust – can arise in a community even when each individual accepts a theory on the basis of biased reasoning, as long as certain conditions are in place.

Consider an example Solomon herself gives, of plate tectonics. There is now a widespread consensus in the geological community that plate tectonics is true, and, given the amazing empirical success of this theory, this seems like a likely candidate for a normative consensus. However, Solomon suggests, the actual process whereby the community came to accept this theory did not involve each individual scientist sitting back and coolly examining the data, but, rather, was shot through with various kinds of biased reasoning. Many scientists came to accept the theory only when evidence was collected within their own sub-discipline, a form of the 'availability bias' (where we overweight evidence which happens to be at hand); there was heavy reliance on individual experience or evidence the experimenters had, themselves, carried out, a form of the 'salience bias'; prior commitments to various theories played a large role in scientists' interpretation of the evidence, a version of the 'confirmation bias' (where we overweight evidence which most fits our prior hypotheses); and, most importantly for our purposes, social pressures and a concern to please authority figures played a role in 'converting' many scientists, but, fortunately, this 'conformity bias' worked to the epistemic good because the authority figures were right. The socially mediated outputs of research processes can be trustworthy, even if individual reasoning is shot through with all sorts of bias.

---

[11] Note that Solomon herself sets out her views much more fully in Solomon, 2007; for introductory purposes, however, it is better to start with her article

Note that Solomon's concern is *not* to provide an account of objectivity as such. Still, her work is clearly relevant as an example of how social interactions between biased agents can mitigate bias. A distinctive feature of Solomon's example is that no-one sat down and explicitly created structures and processes to harness bias to the common good. However, we can draw on such studies as a guide to institutional design. For example, based on our knowledge of social psychology, of the history and sociology of science, and so on, we could identify institutions that tend to combat or harness bias. As such, we can *hope* to create structures that generate trustworthy results. Of course, whether we *succeed* in this task is a different matter, and there are all sorts of cases in which we might worry that social processes can *compound,* rather than *correct,* bias (Kukla, 2012). Still, at least in principle, even if each one of us is subject to all sorts of irremediable bias, it does not follow that the outputs of science must be affected by idiosyncratic factors.

Historically speaking, concepts of objectivity have tended to focus on individual epistemic virtues. There is a reason why Daston and Galison (2007) present their history of objectivity as a history of the 'scientific self'. It should be no surprise, then, that, in practice, we might easily overlook the importance of thinking about the social, and get overly worried about individual biases and failures. Part of the importance of the arguments I have presented in this section is that they allow us to overcome this focus on the individual, which, itself, may be related to the distinctively ethical undertones of trust and objectivity. However, there is also a limitation to the social turn, nicely summarised by Sylvia Culp, 'even when dependence on idiosyncratic presuppositions is eliminated, dependence on the presuppositions shared by the entire community might not be' (Culp, 1995, 440). More bluntly: if everyone is biased, then social interaction won't remove bias. In Section 3, I return to these concerns; first, though, it is useful to consider a second, even more powerful, concern about the simple account of objectivity; however we organise inquiry, justification *must* be value-laden.

2.4 The Simple View of Process Objectivity: the Argument From Inductive Risk

The simple account of objectivity holds that scientific research should not be influenced by, 'want-based' or non-epistemic commitments. I have suggested two kinds of challenges to this view: first, that it is *impossible* for science not to be thus influenced; and, second, that the distinction between epistemic and non-epistemic influences is ill-founded. The previous sub-section considered one version of the first, impossibility, challenge: that scientists, as humans, are invariably influenced by biases and values. I suggested a response to this 'empirical worry': that objective processes should be understood in *social*, rather than *individual*, terms. I will now discuss a different version of the first challenge – that it is, in principle, impossible for justification to be insulated from non-epistemic, want-based factors.

In Section 2.2, I suggested that the simple view of process objectivity is intimately related with the so-called Value Free Ideal. This Ideal has never been uncontroversial; the claim that justification can be free of the influence of all non-epistemic values has been questioned by critics ranging from pragmatists in the 1930s and 1940s, to feminist philosophers in the 1970s and 1980s, to environmental philosophers in the 1990s. However, I will focus on a set of challenges centred around the 'argument from inductive risk' (AIR).[12] I focus on this argument because it is dialectically powerful. Many arguments against the Value Free Ideal are premised on the claim that it is impossible to distinguish 'epistemic' from 'non-epistemic' considerations. These are important worries, which I discuss in the next section. However, they may be dialectically weak against a hardcore defender of the Value Free Ideal, who will just reply that, although it may be *difficult* to distinguish epistemic from non-epistemic, it is not impossible to do so. The power of the AIR is that it purports to show that even if we hold a strict demarcation between the epistemic and the non-epistemic, science reasoning *must* be value-laden. It is a fascinating instance of judo epistemology, where you use your opponent's strength against her.

The first major statement of the AIR was offered by Richard Rudner in 1953 (Rudner, 1953). Its current influence stems, however, mainly from the work of Heather Douglas (2000, 2009). Although there are important differences between Rudner's formulation and Douglas' formulation (and various reworked versions in light of criticisms), the broad shape of the argument runs as follows:

> Scientists accept or reject hypotheses.
> Typically, these hypotheses are not deductively entailed by the available evidence.
> As such, scientists face 'problems of inductive risk': they risk accepting hypotheses which are, in fact, false or rejecting hypotheses which are, in fact, true.
> There is no (responsible) way to set the trade-off between false positives and false negatives other than by appeal to the non-epistemic costs associated with acting on different types of error.
> Therefore, scientists *must* appeal to ethical values in scientific inference.

To make this argument vivid, consider a super-simplified example (adapted from Rudner). Imagine that we have purchased a machine for manufacturing

---

[12] Note that even this recent round of debate seems to mirror an earlier set of debates from the 1950s

belt buckles. We want to know whether the machine reliably produces faultless buckles. To test this, we run the machine a certain number of times and check the belt buckles for faults. Imagine, now, two scenarios: in one, the buckles will be used for belts to hold up trousers; in the other, the buckles will be used to strap babies into car seats. Plausibly, we would, and should, test the machine's products many more times in the latter case than in the former. While there are some costs to people wearing belts which are not, in fact, properly fastened – the embarrassment of having your trousers fall down in public – these costs are minimal when compared with the costs of babies being strapped into cars with malfunctioning buckles. More formally: it seems we have strong ethical reasons to vary the amount of evidence we require before accepting that the machine is working properly in proportion to the disvalue of the non-epistemic consequences of epistemic error.

Although the belt buckle example is simplistic, many writers have argued that many aspects of actual scientific practice are structurally analogous: we must decide how much evidence to require before accepting claims, and such decisions turn, in part, on the non-epistemic consequences of error. For example, in her influential paper reintroducing inductive risk concerns to the literature, Heather Douglas (2000) shows how research into carcinogenicity can be reconstructed as involving a series of judgements about how to trade-off different 'inductive risks'. This is most obvious in statistical testing: in setting a 'p value' for accepting some hypothesis. The lower our p value, the less likely we are to accept that a chemical is carcinogenic when, in fact, it is not – that is, the lower our risk of a false positive – but the more likely we are to fail to accept that a chemical is carcinogenic when, in fact, it is – that is, the higher our risk of a false negative (for an early version of these worries, see Churchman, 1948). Less obviously, Douglas suggests that similar decisions arise throughout testing; for example, it is not always clear whether to categorise some image on a slide as a tumour or not. In resolving these ambiguous cases, then, medical researchers must balance two kinds of error, categorising images as representing tumours when, in fact, they do not, and not categorising images as representing tumours when, in fact, they do. Again, plausibly, these epistemic decisions should be guided by a concern with the non-epistemic costs of error; whether the consequences of 'under-counting' tumours are worse than those of 'over-counting' them.

You could, of course, dispute aspects of Douglas' argument. It is important, though, to keep an eye on the overall problem the AIR raises: as soon as we agree that at least some aspects of scientific reasoning involve making some leap beyond the available evidence, and, hence, some risk of a false positive, we face a challenge: why run *this* particular level of epistemic risk, rather than a higher or lower level? For example, why tolerate a 5 per cent risk of a false positive result – as when 'p' values are set at 0.05, rather than, say, a 1 per cent risk or a 10 per cent risk; why prefer to categorise ambiguous images as tumours rather than not? *Prima facie*, it is unclear that there can be any straightforwardly *epistemic* response to this kind of question; categorising the image as a tumour risks misrepresenting the world, but so, too, does not categorising the image as a tumour. Furthermore, such choices *can* have important, non-epistemic consequences; for example, under-counting the number of tumours may lead us to under-estimate the rate of cancer in the population, and, hence, to under-regulate a dangerous substance. As such, it seems to follow that a key aspect of scientific reasoning – balancing epistemic risks – can and should be guided by ethical concerns.

Before going on, it is useful to remind the reader how the AIR relates to the general topic of objectivity. We can understand the simple view of process objectivity, and the associated Value Free Ideal, as assuming that certain forms of reasoning – for example, following the norms of Bayesian confirmation theory – are, broadly, truth-tropic, but certain influences on reasoning – for example, appeal to political values – are non-truth-tropic. The AIR points to a problem: strictly, the evidence will always *underdetermine* acceptance of hypotheses. Therefore, non-epistemic values are needed to decide how certain we must be in some claim to be 'certain enough' to accept it. Note that the AIR does not hold that value considerations can or should *replace* epistemic considerations. For example, a proponent can happily admit that, say, epidemiological techniques are epistemically preferable to astrology as tools for making predictions, insofar as they produce both fewer false positives *and* fewer false negatives. Therefore, scientists should use epidemiological techniques, rather than astrology, even if the latter would fit better with some non-epistemic concerns. Rather, her concern is that even the best techniques do not deliver certainty, and, as such, any decision about accepting claims on the basis of evidence essentially involves non-epistemic value judgements. As such, if science does involve accepting claims, then our decisions must be made using non-epistemic values. The proper role for values is 'indirect' – setting thresholds for acceptance – rather than 'direct' – telling us what to believe – but, still, a proper role. The argument posits an *in principle* objection to the claim that scientific reasoning *can* proceed without appeal to non-epistemic values.

In turn, the AIR provides a more general template for denying the Value Free Ideal (and, hence, the simple view of objectivity): identify *some* unavoidable step in the scientific research process which is underdetermined and you find a possible role for non-epistemic values. For example, consider an argument from David Ludwig (2015), extending a version of the AIR from epistemology to ontology. Ludwig suggests that many scientific practices require some kind of 'ontology', that is, some way of cutting the world up into types of things. However, Ludwig argues that the world itself does not come pre-packaged in ontological types. For example, ecology requires ways of distinguishing different species, but the world itself underdetermines precisely how we should divide living beings into different species. We must make 'ontological choices' – choices about how to categorise the world – which are underdetermined, in the sense that they cannot be guided solely by factual considerations. In turn, these ontological choices have important ethical consequences. For example, a decision about how to categorise the living world into species might have important implications for findings about the degree of biodiversity in some habitat, and, hence for policy-making. Therefore, Ludwig argues, ethical values do and should play a role in resolving ontological underdetermination.[13]

There are various ambiguities in inductive risk arguments (for example, over the precise sense in which scientists 'must' appeal to non-epistemic values). There are worries about whether the argument can be extended in the way authors such as Ludwig propose. However, these issues are most easily understood in terms of various possible responses to the argument. Therefore, rather than clarify *precisely* what the AIR shows here, I will, instead, move straight onto possible responses, and discuss the ambiguities as we go along.

At a very abstract level, we can identify four possible responses to the AIR:

1) To deny scientists make inductive leaps at all, such that we can continue to hold the standard view of objectivity and the Value Free Ideal
2) To accept that scientists make inductive leaps, but redefine concepts of 'bias', 'influence' and so on in such a way as to retain a version of the standard view of objectivity
3) To accept that the argument works, and to redefine objectivity in terms of having only certain sorts of values influence science in certain sorts of ways[14]
4) To give up entirely on the concept of objectivity.

---

[13] There is a tricky issue here: in standard inductive risk cases, it seems that there is a pretty straightforward sense in which a decision to accept claims can be wrong, because true or false, whereas in the 'ontological choice' case, matters are not so straightforward. For this kind of reason, Biddle and Kukla (2017) have stressed the importance of distinguishing 'inductive risk' in the strict sense from the broader class of 'epistemic risks'. I agree entirely that it is often important to distinguish different forms of underdetermination, but, as I explain below, drawing these distinctions does not undermine the general thrust of Douglas' arguments

[14] This is an intentionally vague characterisation, because there is no shortage of options here: for example, you might think that objectivity is secured by ensuring that only 'correct' values influence science (where 'correct' might mean 'true' or 'democratically legitimate' or ...); alternatively, you might think that what secures objectivity is not that certain sorts of values (the right ones or true ones) are used, but *how* those values enter into justification (say, they must

In the rest of this section, I will consider versions of strategies 1) and 2). The next section outlines one way in which we might attempt 3), and the final section considers some versions of 4).

2.5 Responding to Inductive Risk Concerns 1: Do Scientists Accept Claims at All?

The most important response to inductive risk arguments in the recent literature has been made by Gregor Betz (2013). Betz mounts his defence on the case-study of climate science. This is an excellent example: climate science is, of course, implicated in heated social, political and economic debates. In actual debates over climate change, it is common to read accusation that both climate scientists and climate sceptics have allowed their non-epistemic commitments to colour their claims. Typically, however, such accusations are taken to point to a *problem* with their reasoning; if the AIR is correct, then it seems that such accusations and responses to them lose their bite. Imagine, for example, a right-winger who attacks climate science as a left-wing project and, as such, not something the right should take seriously. The AIR seems to imply that they may have a point. For example, perhaps climate scientists calibrated their tolerance for errors in ways which reflected a set of 'leftist' values, such that 'rightists' can ignore the scientists' claims on broadly political grounds. Regardless of one's politics, this kind of result seems problematic. Surely, we need *some* common ground for political debate, and objective science is an obvious candidate.

With this background in place, consider the work of the Intergovernmental Panel on Climate Change (IPCC). The IPCC was set up in 1993 to:

> assess on a comprehensive, objective, open and transparent basis the scientific, technical and socio-economic information relevant to understanding the scientific basis of risk of human-induced climate change, its potential impacts and options for adaptation and mitigation. IPCC reports should be neutral with respect to policy, although they may need to deal objectively with scientific, technical and socio-economic factors relevant to the application of particular policies (IPCC, 1998).

There are many fascinating aspects of the IPCC. For current purposes, we only need to focus on one of these aspects, that, in their voluminous reports, only one claim is made outright: that the climate is warming. Every other claim in IPCC reports has an explicit epistemic qualifier: for example, that it is 'almost certain' that such changes are anthropogenic, and 'very likely' that such changes will have significant impacts.

---

never over-ride epistemic concerns, or they must enter in a transparent manner). For a useful overview of some of the complexities here, see Schroeder, 2017

Why is this important? Remember the first premise of the AIR: that scientists accept or reject claims. In the initial round of debate prompted by Rudner's work, Richard Jeffrey (1956) opposed this premise, suggesting, instead, that scientists might simply report the 'degree-of-support' which hypotheses enjoy. If so, then, strictly, scientists do not accept claims, and, as such, they never run inductive risks in the first place. As Betz points out, we can see the IPCC as doing something very similar to Jeffrey's proposed strategy: rather than report 'bald hypotheses' – that is, straight-out claims about the world – instead, it reports 'hedged hypotheses' – that is, claims about the likelihood of certain sorts of hypotheses, given the evidence. In turn, reporting 'hedged hypotheses' does not involve going beyond the available evidence; rather, it is a kind of summary of what the available evidence says. If so, scientists do not 'need' – in either a logical or moral sense – to appeal to non-epistemic values to solve problems of inductive risk, because they do not solve problems of inductive risk at all. They hand the problem over to their audiences. (Interestingly, Betz suggests that this kind of division-of-labour between scientists and policy-makers fits well with broader ethical norms of respect for autonomy and political norms of democratic decision-making – as an aside, it is important to note that arguments *for* value-free science may, themselves, be motivated by broadly political concerns.) For Betz, science *can* be objective as long as scientists do what the IPCC (apparently) does – just avoid making inductive leaps altogether!

Before going on, note two things. First, of course, Betz's claim here is not that all *actual* science is *actually* value-free. Maybe some scientists do make inductive leaps, hence embroiling themselves in value judgements. Rather, his claim is that, as the IPCC case demonstrates, even extremely politically relevant science *can* be value-free (and that this is a good thing). In turn, we might expand his strategy by thinking about other cases that also involve reporting hedged hypotheses, rather than bald hypotheses. For example, many scientific research papers will often report results as established at some confidence interval; on a Betz-inspired account, these reporting strategies are not merely window-dressing, but central to avoiding an embroilment of the epistemic and the ethical. Second, as we noted above, there are many variants on the basic AIR. Strictly, Betz's response to the inductive risk argument does not respond to these variations. However, we can imagine ways in which his argumentative strategy might be extended to these cases ('given this way of individuating species – and note that others are available – there are precisely 10 species in these wetlands').

Betz surely has an important point that there are good democratic reasons why, in general, it is preferable for scientists to report uncertainties as clearly as possible to policy-makers, rather than to make value judgements themselves. If we do not hold this distinction, then we immediately get caught up in a very tricky debate over which values scientists should use to solve inductive risk problems (Schroeder, 2017). Unfortunately, it is not clear that his strategy for salvaging value-freedom is successful.

First, Katie Steele (2012) has argued that the presentation of scientific results in probabilistic form may involve making value judgements. Scientists at the IPCC face interesting problems in translating their coarse-grained probability estimates into standardised protocols for representing uncertainties. Plausibly, in responding to these problems, they have to make decisions that resemble inductive risk problems; for example, when it is unclear whether to report that they are 'almost certain' of some claim or whether it is merely 'very likely', they must decide whether it is worse to overstate or understate their degree-of-confidence. Second, as I have argued, scientists at the IPCC face significant difficulties in deciding *which* evidence to base their estimates on, for example in cases involving research which has yet to be peer-reviewed (John, 2015). Plausibly, these decisions resemble inductive risk cases, in that scientists face a choice between using only the 'best' evidence, hence risking overlooking some good evidence, and using 'all' the evidence, hence including some 'bad' evidence.

On the face of it, both these concerns may seem very specific to Betz's case-study. However, they point to broader worries. Steele's worry is that there may be significant second-order uncertainty about how uncertain we should be, such that any attempt to communicate uncertainty always involves a kind of inductive risk problem. My concern is that even when we report our confidence conditional on some body-of-evidence, we must make choices about how to construct that body-of-evidence. The general lesson here is simple: that epistemic underdetermination occurs in so many different ways at so many different levels and stages of scientific reasoning, that it may be (practically) impossible for scientists to avoid taking inductive risks. Even when results are presented as hedged rather than bald hypotheses, this presentation may hide a huge number of ways in which scientists have 'gone beyond' the evidence. Of course, there are ways in which defenders of the simple view of objectivity can respond to these problems. However, there are good reasons to think that scientists cannot avoid making inductive leaps simply by sticking caveats in front of their conclusions.

2.6 Responding to Inductive Risk Concerns 2: Conventions, Values and Objectivity

One way of summarising the Value Free Ideal is as the claim that scientific justification can and should be free of 'biases', understood as an umbrella term to mean any non-epistemic factors. The AIR poses a challenge to the ideal because it implies that, whenever scientists make inductive leaps, non-epistemic factors must play a role in justification. Betz's response to this argument is to deny that scientists do make inductive leaps. However, this is a tricky position to defend. An alternative response, then, is to concede that scientists make inductive leaps, but to define 'bias' in such a way that not all inductive leaps involve the influence of bias. If so, we can hold that scientists do solve inductive risk problems, but deny that this implies all science is biased. If objectivity is a lack of bias, science can be objective even if scientists make inductive leaps. I will now discuss one version of this general strategy, by appeal to the notion of methodological conventions. This response is interesting both for its own sake, and because it returns us to a key theme from the end of Section 1: the relationship between purely procedural objectivity and scientific objectivity.

To get a rough grasp on this response, consider the initial round of debates around inductive risk. Rudner's own formulation of his conclusion is as the claim that the scientist '*qua* scientist' makes value judgements. There is an obvious response to Rudner's conclusion, first suggested by Isaac Levi (1960), that the scientist can simply follow conventional rules to resolve inductive risk problems. As such, she need not make any value judgements herself at all. One possible response to Levi's claim is that the individual scientist ought not follow rules slavishly, but has a moral obligation to consider the non-epistemic consequences of error. Imagine, for example, that you are working at the buckle factory. One day, the management switches production from belt buckles to car seat buckles, but does not change the standard protocol for testing machines' reliability. Plausibly, you ought to demand that the conventions are changed, because, in this case, they seem out of kilter with ethical demands. This response is interesting, but generates a new problem: does the AIR aim to show that scientists *must* make value judgements in a logical sense or in an ethical sense? That is, is the argument intended to show that, given the problem of underdetermination, there is *no way* of doing science which does not involve scientists making value judgements, or, rather, that scientists have a *moral obligation* to reflect on the ways in which their conventional epistemic standards might have non-epistemic consequences?

To disentangle some of these issues, consider some proposals by Torsten Wilholt (2009, 2012), responding to Douglas' work. Wilholt agrees with Douglas that scientific justification *does* involve making inductive leaps. However, similarly to Levi, he also holds that there are various 'conventional' standards that determine which leaps scientists ought to make. We can, then, define 'biased' research as research that deviates from these conventional epistemic standards. If Wilholt is right, scientific justification can both involve solving inductive risk problems and be objective, just as long as scientists solve their problems using conventional standards.

One important aspect of this response is that it helps us make sense of various familiar concerns about objectivity, while acknowledging the force of inductive risk arguments. Consider cases in which 'interested' researchers – such as those at a pharmaceutical company – make inductive leaps in some way that seems designed to improve their chances of showing that some claim is true. Wilholt provides a fascinating case-study of this phenomenon: in testing whether bisphenol-A has harmful side effects, it seems that industry researchers used rat species which are known to be less sensitive to oestrogen, hence leading to a far lower rate of side effects being discovered in industry-funded studies than in non-industry-funded research (Wilholt, 2009). On the face of it, this looks like a paradigm case of biased, non-objective research. However, phrasing this concern is difficult. It is unclear that there is any straightforwardly *epistemic* reason against using a particular rat species for medical experimentation; in a nice phrase from Quill R Kukla (writing as Rebecca Kukla), it is not as if which rat species to use in experiments is written 'in the book of nature' (Kukla, 2012). Wilholt's proposal provides a way of avoiding this mess: even if there is no straightforwardly epistemic reason to use one rat species rather than another, if the researchers' choice of species was not in line with conventional standards, their research was non-objective.

Unfortunately, there is an obvious concern with going conventional as a way of saving objectivity talk: that it seems to risk collapsing into what, above, I called a purely procedural account of objectivity. Of course, we can understand scientific objectivity in terms of blindly following rules, but this does not tell us anything about why the results of following procedures in this way should be thought epistemically trustworthy. To make this point vivid, consider a silly example. Serious astrologers follow complex rules to guide their predictive practices. Given these rules, certain predictions are proper, others are improper. Consider an astrologer who follows these rules, even when doing so is not in her interests – 'I'm sorry, easily angered monarch, but you will lose the battle tomorrow' – and one who bends these rules to her own interests – 'the stars say you will win, oh brave King'. The former astrologer is objective in a way in which the latter is not. Still, most of us would think that, epistemically speaking, both sets of predictions are worthless. Consider, now, the more serious example of biomedical research. Even if it is true that an industry-sponsored trial diverges from conventional epistemic standards, it is not clear why that fact should affect our *epistemic trust* of the trial's results, unless we have an independent account of why following the standards is epistemically preferable in the first place.

Wilholt has an answer to this challenge.[15] He holds that there is a broadly epistemic justification for conventional standards. Efficient and effective scientific communication requires that scientists have shared standards for resolving inductive risk problems; as such, conventional standards enable and sustain trust and communication inside the scientific community (Wilholt, 2012). A nice feature of Wilholt's argument is that it resolves the odd ambiguity in inductive risk arguments noted above, over whether the argument is intended to point to logical or ethical issues. For Wilholt, the individual scientist can avoid making value judgements herself – she just follows the conventions – and there are good reasons to hold by the standards even when their non-epistemic consequences are worrying – that doing so is necessary to sustain the scientific enterprise more generally.

Still, although Wilholt's argument is ingenious, it is not clear that it resolves the worries raised by the AIR. It certainly seems correct to say, as Wilholt does, that having fixed epistemic standards is important for all sorts of broadly epistemic reasons. In turn, we might note that these epistemic consequences are also non-epistemically valuable, insofar as we value the non-epistemic consequences of a well-functioning scientific community. Still, this consideration does not, in and of itself, show that we have epistemic reasons to prefer any specific set of standards over any other. For example, it may be true that epistemic communities which employ statistical testing tend to function far better if everyone uses the *same* 'p value'; it does not follow, however, that there are epistemic reasons to favour, say, $p = 0.05$, rather than $p = 0.01$ or $p = 0.1$. However, we might still be able to offer non-epistemic reasons for or against these conventions. For example, we might worry that, in the context of pharmaceutical testing, using $p = 0.1$ would be too likely to lead us to accept false claims, hence harming patients, whereas using $p = 0.01$ would be too likely to lead us to fail to accept true claims, hence foregoing helping patients, and so on.

My point here is not to settle which conventions we should use. Rather, it is more general: even if there is an *epistemic* argument for having conventions *at all*, it is unlikely that there is an epistemic argument for any *particular* convention. Indeed, one way of understanding the AIR is that, from a purely epistemological point-of-view, any particular way of trading-off different kinds of epistemic errors is arbitrary. However, this does not mean that all ways of trading-off epistemic risks are equally acceptable from a *non-epistemic* perspective. Rather, certain conventions for trading-off inductive risks may be seen as implicitly endorsing, codifying or promoting non-epistemic value

---

[15] Note that so, too, did Levi (1960), but his response seems to rely on an implausible assumption about the long-term goals of science

judgements. (Note that this can happen regardless of *why* or *how* those conventions arose, and regardless of whether anyone ever really reflects on this. By analogy, the practice of meat eating arose for all sorts of reasons which did not involve ethical reflection, and most meat eaters do not reflect on their meat eating – still, it is plausible to say that people who eat meat endorse an ethical view on the relative value of animal life.)

In turn, these concerns seem relevant to assessing the trustworthiness of scientists' claims: if some audience member denies the value judgements implicit in some convention, then she seems to have reasons not to trust claims which are established relative to those conventions (Irzik and Kurtulmus, 2019). Notions of objectivity are, as we saw in Section 1, bound up with notions of trust. If so, it seems that an account of full objectivity needs to go beyond adherence with conventions to engage with the question of whether the conventions can be non-epistemically justified. Of course, there are various ways of spelling out what we mean by 'non-epistemically justified' here. The key point, however, is simple: if we accept that scientists make inductive leaps, then non-epistemic value judgements may be necessary for, rather than distortions of, trustworthy science, and, hence, objectivity.[16]

2.7 Conclusions

In Section 1, I outlined three conditions for an account of objectivity: that it should match our everyday use of having something to do with notions of accurate representation, that it should pick out something valuable and that it should be viable. In this section, I have explored the simple view of process objectivity, where processes are objective to the extent that they are not influenced by various 'want-based influences': biases, interests and non-epistemic values. How does this fare against our desiderata?

It is trivial to say that isolating representation practices from our wants is linked to notions of accurate representation. Unfortunately, defending and developing the simple view beyond this truism requires us to do two things: to be able to draw a distinction between 'epistemic' and 'non-epistemic' influences, and to hold that it is possible for justificatory practices to be influenced only by the former, and not the latter. I placed the first issue to one side, to focus on the second. Broadly, there are two worries about the claim that scientific processes can be insulated from non-epistemic values: first, that, as a human activity, scientific practice is bound to be influenced by non-epistemic values; second, that it is, in principle, impossible to engage in justification

---

[16] See John, 2019 for my preferred way of spelling out and responding to these concerns, but the general worry is far more significant and general than my attempt to resolve them

without appeal to non-epistemic values. We have already outlined a response to the first challenge: to focus attention on *social processes* of objectivity. However, the second challenge, which I linked to the AIR, is harder to defuse: it challenges both the *viability* and the *value* of value-free justification. Maybe scientists *must* (implicitly) make value judgements; even if you deny this, given the non-epistemic costs of error, they *ought* to do so. Of course, there are responses to this argument, but, as we saw, neither Betz nor Wilholt clearly succeeds in defending a viable and valuable account of objectivity in response to inductive risk concerns.

In short, we face a dilemma: it seems that value-freedom is central to objectivity, but value-free justification seems chimerical. Maybe we need to accept that non-epistemic values play some role in science, and find a way of deciding which values are apt to do so?

3 Values, Diversity and Debate

In this section, I will explore how these concerns relate to Longino's influential account of objectivity, which, in turn, questions the epistemic/non-epistemic distinction itself. To set the scene, I will first discuss Elisabeth Lloyd's fascinating discussion of 'bias' in the case of research into the female orgasm.

3.1 Bias: the Case of the Female Orgasm

There is a plausible evolutionary explanation of the male orgasm. Roughly, the physical pleasure of orgasm provides men with an incentive to have penetrative sex, and, thus, increase their reproductive fitness. As such, it is easy to tell a story of how mammalian males came to have the trait of a capacity to orgasm; this is a highly advantageous adaptation. By contrast, there is far more disagreement over the evolution of the female orgasm, because there is no obvious correlate to the ejaculation of sperm. In a highly influential study, Lloyd (2005) considers 20 attempts to account for the evolution of the female orgasm. The vast majority seek to explain the female orgasm as an adaptation which improves reproductive fitness. For example, the 'sperm suction' account posits that, during orgasm, vaginal muscles clench to 'suck' the sperm towards the fallopian tubes (Lloyd, 2005, 179). Unfortunately, as Lloyd shows, these accounts are hopelessly at odds with the rest of our scientific knowledge; many of them are simply physiologically implausible; they conflict with what we know about sexual behaviour in other mammalian species; and they do not fit with demographic studies of human sexual response and behaviour (Lloyd, 2005, chapter 2). Lloyd's work is extremely rich, but a simple example helps get across her strategy: we know that most women are far more likely to orgasm from clitoral simulation rather than from penetrative sex; as such, it seems highly unlikely that the capacity to orgasm has much to do with reproductive success.

Rather, Lloyd suggests that the only plausible account is one initially offered by Donald Symons, that the female orgasm is a by-product of the evolution of the male orgasm (Lloyd, 2005, chapter 5). To explain, Lloyd agrees that the male orgasm can be explained as an evolutionary adaptation. However, the foetus develops a proto-penis before sex differentiation occurs. Post-differentiation, men go on to develop a penis, whereas women develop a clitoris. The penis serves an evolutionary function, but the clitoris does not – it is simply a by-product of evolution. (It may help to think about a related example. There is a plausible evolutionary account of why women have nipples: this allows them to feed infants, promoting fitness. Male nipples, by contrast, are non-functional. Why, then, do men have nipples? Again, the reason is simply that sex differentiation occurs only after the foetus starts to develop nipples.)

Although the by-product account of the female orgasm fits best with the rest of our data, it is extremely unpopular in the literature. Lloyd explains this in terms of two 'biases' which structure research (Lloyd, 2005, chapter 8). First, there is an *adaptationist* bias; that is, a background assumption in evolutionary research that *all* traits are explicable in terms of past contribution to evolutionary fitness. Clearly, this bias then serves to stack the deck against the 'by-product' account. However, even hardcore adaptationists are willing to accept that some traits – such as male nipples – may not be evolutionary adaptations. Lloyd suggests, then, that a second important factor in the case of female orgasm research is an 'androcentric bias', that is, a background assumption that female sexual response must resemble male sexual response. For men, orgasm is a central aspect of sexual pleasure, and, hence, key to understanding male sexual behaviour; researchers assume, then, that something similar must be true of women, and work their theories accordingly. Men are treated as the standard case and women as deviations from the basic blueprint. Lloyd claims that the combination of the adaptationist and androcentric biases leads researchers systematically to overlook the most empirically plausible evolutionary story.

In using the term bias, Lloyd is *not* claiming that researchers are *deliberately* twisting or manipulating data. Plausibly, many of the researchers under discussion would not even be aware of the relevant biases or of their effects on their research. Rather, her claim is that the ways in which the phenomenon of the female orgasm is treated as an object of scientific study, the ways it is investigated and what evidence is considered, are all structured by a series of implicit, questionable assumptions, both about biological theory and about what sexual pleasure is (or ought to be).

(Before leaving the detail of Lloyd's work, it is helpful to consider the reception of her claims. Lloyd herself thinks of her work as developing a broadly feminist agenda, focused on showing how evolutionary research has treated men as the normal or standard case. However, some critics have attacked her feminist credentials, on the grounds that her account implies that female sexual response is 'secondary' to male sexual response. Lloyd has fought back, arguing that to interpret her work as diminishing female sexuality is a version of the adaptationist bias, according to which only selected-for traits are important or valuable. She memorably suggests that the by-product account should be renamed the 'fantastic bonus' account! This odd story serves as an example of a more general lesson, that the political, ethical or social implications of scientific findings are rarely straightforward. Whether a claim is empowering or dismissive is very much in the eye of the beholder. It is best to be sceptical of sweeping claims about the political valence of a research project; someone, somewhere will take offence at a project.)

How does Lloyd's fascinating story relate to the concerns about 'value-freedom' and objectivity discussed in Section 2? One important point is that precisely because the relevant biases are widely shared across the research field, interaction between researchers will not necessarily lead the biases to be exposed or recognised. In the plate tectonics example, Solomon shows how individual biases may be cancelled out through social interaction. By contrast, the biases which Lloyd explores are themselves 'social': the problem is not that individual thought processes depart from rational ideals, but with the operation of an entire research field. The second important point is that Lloyd's biases affect research before we get to the problem of inductive risk. In setting up inductive risk cases, I assumed that there was a clear, straightforward way of calculating the probabilities of hypotheses conditional on some body-of-evidence; the problem of 'bias' emerged because different agents might disagree over how certain is 'certain enough' for acceptance of claims. By contrast, Lloyd's case shows how both our evidence and our hypotheses might themselves be shaped by various sorts of commitments. Third, and most importantly, on Lloyd's story, it is hard, however, to sort these commitments neatly into an 'epistemic' pile and a 'non-epistemic' pile; an adaptationist stance is more like a bet about what the world *might* be like than a claim which is itself based on the evidence; androcentric attitudes are not simply misogynistic dislike of women, but shape a more general understanding of the world. Both commitments are *pre*-epistemic: they provide a framework within which to formulate hypotheses and interpret evidence. It is hard, though, to see how we might investigate the world at all without any such commitments. Lloyd's claim, then, is that *these* commitments are problematic *in this case*, and should be replaced by *others*; it is not that *all* pre-epistemic commitments are inherently problematic. Plausibly, without some pre-epistemic commitments, we could not get to the epistemic at all.

3.2 Going Deeply Social: Longino

As Section 2 explored, the notion that objectivity is linked to an absence of non-epistemic values or biases seems appealing. However, the AIR poses a serious challenge to this idea. Therefore, either we need a refutation of the inductive risk argument – which, I claimed, is no easy task – or we need to rethink objectivity. The case-study above suggests a second problem for the standard view of objectivity: that background assumptions are necessary for doing scientific work at all, but these pre-epistemic commitments look very similar to biases.

The 'simple view' of objectivity is beset by problems, but can we do any better? Perhaps the most influential way of thinking through the problem of pre-epistemic commitments, and related issues around the epistemic/non-epistemic distinction, has been offered by Helen Longino.[17] In turn, Longino's general strategy, to offer a deeply social account of objectivity based on a notion of critical dialogue, provides one template for thinking about how we might respond to other concerns about objectivity and biases, such as those explored in the previous section. In this section, then, I shall sketch Longino's 'contextual empiricist' project. Before doing so, two notes may help the reader. First, there is a historical oddity in my presentation. Chronologically speaking, Longino's work predates lots of the work we have discussed so far, but is, in many ways, far more radical. Second, often Longino's positive account of objectivity is presented as a kind of free-standing proposal that chimes well with contemporary political and ethical concerns about the importance of diversity. It is clear why such moves are appealing. However, they can be problematic; first, because they overlook potential ambiguities and tensions in notions of diversity (Harding, 2015, xi); second, because they overlook the deep theoretical basis of Longino's work, making it seem as if we can just easily slot her work into any old epistemic framework. Therefore, I start my exposition with Longino's general philosophical picture, rather than just giving her conclusions.

---

[17] Longino has developed her views over a series of books, but, for current purposes, I focus on the highly influential presentation in Longino, 1990. Interested readers should also consult Longino, 2002 and 2013

Longino's arguments for contextual empiricism start from a distinction she draws between two accounts of the relationship between data and theory: on a 'syntactic' view (which she equates with positivism), there are logical relationships of confirmation or refutation between data and theory; the alternative, 'wholism' (which Longino equates with Kuhn's work) holds, by contrast, that theory and data are mutually supporting (Longino, 1990, chapter 3). Unfortunately, neither approach works. The 'syntactic' approach fails because data reports are theory-laden: we cannot *just* look to the logical (*syntactic*) relations between theory and data, because data reports only confirm/disconfirm in virtue of agreed meanings (*semantics*, given by theory). The wholist recognises this fact, but faces a different challenge, that she cannot account for disagreement: if *my* theory determines *my* data, and *your* theory *your* data, then how can we ever disagree over whose theory best fits the data? Longino's solution to this very general problem is to split the difference: she thinks that *data* only become *evidence* for or against a theory in light of other assumptions (*contra* the syntactic view), but holds that the relevant assumptions need not be those of the theory under consideration (*contra* the wholist).[18]

So far, so neat. The key move comes in Longino's account of the assumptions – or, as she calls them, 'values' – which structure the move from data to evidence to theory. Longino draws a distinction between *constitutive* values – goals or ends which make a human endeavour what it is – and *contextual* values – considerations which are applied or used in pursuit of that endeavour. For Longino, scientific inquiry is guided by two constitutive values: *truth* and *knowledge*. (You might think that these two are broadly synonymous, but Longino does not, as she uses 'knowledge' in a slightly unusual sense to mean something like useful claims which need not be literally true.) Unfortunately, aiming at these endpoints is insufficient to guide scientific inference. We also need 'contextual values', which we can understand as assumptions that guide us in the process of turning our data into evidence.

Some of Longino's own examples help grasp the concept of contextual values, which may be more or less field-specific. In evolutionary anthropology, an assumption of 'man the hunter, woman the gatherer' is, she claims, often used to guide the interpretation of findings (Longino, 1990, 106–110). In hormonal research, there is a strong preference for interpreting data using linear models of causation, rather than models which allow for feedback (Longino,

---

[18] Readers interested in the general philosophy of science might note that Lloyd is also a leading proponent of the 'semantic' account of theories (see Lloyd, 1998); as I noted above, it is not clear that we can extract any account of objectivity from a broader philosophical web. For a helpful historical account of the relationship between various trends in philosophy of science and a growing awareness of the role of the 'social' in inference, see Zammito, 2004

1990, chapter 7). At the most abstract level, scientists are often claimed to prefer simpler, over more complex theories (Longino, 1996). Beyond Longino's own examples, we can understand both the 'adaptationist' and 'androcentric' biases Lloyd identifies as 'contextual values', which provide a frame for interpreting data about the female orgasm.

In the previous section, I talked about 'non-epistemic values'; for example, justice or well-being. That term implies that there might be 'epistemic values': that is to say, goods whose value is related to our distinctively epistemic, as opposed to ethical aims. Indeed, many defenders of the Value Free Ideal admit that problems of scientific inference are sometimes based on *more* than the evidence; what they claim, however, is that we can close this gap using 'epistemic', rather than 'non-epistemic' values (McMullin, 1982). For example, some theorists claim that, when choosing between two hypotheses, both of which are equally well-supported by the evidence, we should choose the hypothesis which is 'simpler', because there is *some* link between simplicity and truth. From this perspective, then, we might think of Longino's 'contextual values' as proper when (but only when) they are 'epistemic' values.

Central to Longino's project, however, is the claim that contextual values cannot be understood or justified in purely 'epistemic' terms, but, rather, invariably encode and reflect non-epistemic value judgements. For example, it is not difficult to see that the 'man the hunter, woman the gatherer' model is not itself a straightforwardly epistemic commitment, but seem to reify and normalise contemporary social norms. Indeed, Longino has suggested that even such paradigmatic 'epistemic' values as 'simplicity' may reflect a distinctively 'male' perspective (Longino, 1996). Of course, other cases are more complex; for example, at first glance, it is not clear that an adaptationist bias in evolutionary research reflects any substantive ethical or political judgements. Nonetheless, it is clear that these kinds of commitments cannot straightforwardly be justified in purely epistemic terms. Rather, they are chosen, at least in part, for a mishmash of epistemic and practical reasons, say expediency or familiarity. We could, of course, insist that, if we were dogged enough, we could find some epistemic basis for all of our contextual values. Nonetheless, it is not clear that we couldn't find equally good epistemic justifications for using other contextual values. As such, we might well worry that there is no simple set of purely 'epistemic' values which might guide inference.

We now seem to face a problem: contextual values are necessary for doing science, and contextual values are not purely epistemic. If we think of non-epistemic value judgements as something like brute preferences, then, it seems, scientific objectivity is threatened, because want-based commitments will invariably shape scientific work. However, Longino suggests, contextual values can themselves be assessed as better or worse through a process of reasoning and deliberation, where they are exposed to criticism – both epistemic and ethical – by the community as a whole. Specifically, she suggests that the results of scientific inquiry constitute objective knowledge if, and only if, it allows for 'transformative criticism' (Longino, 1990, 76). The possibility of such criticism requires that four conditions are met:

a. there are venues for open criticism; for example, journals provide space for critics to point to problems in scientists' contextual values
b. there is uptake of criticism; that is, scientists listen to critics, consider what they say and, if convinced, change their practices
c. there are public standards for assessment of evidence and of criticism (which, in turn, can shift in publicly accessible ways across time); that is, it is clear to all what kinds of criticisms are well-made, and what sorts of responses are appropriate
d. there is tempered equality of intellectual standing between scientists and critics; for example, scientists listen to critics, rather than dismissing them out of hand.

Longino thinks that science must be grounded in data – and, hence, is an empiricist – but, also, that we must take account of contextual values; hence, she calls her position 'contextual empiricism'. Consider, again, the case of research on the female orgasm: plausibly, that research would be better were we to broaden the community of inquiry. Importantly, this broadening would include listening not only to what we might think of as 'scientific' dissent on the status of adaptationism in evolutionary theory, but also 'political' dissent, for example from feminist scholars challenging assumptions that male sexual response is 'normal'. Precisely because much of Longino's work, and related work, is critical of current practice, it is important to note that Longino's claim is *not* that opening up dialogue will *always* lead us to re-evaluate our scientific theories. Rather, her claim is that, for scientific results to be objective, there must be some process which allows for debate and possible uptake to occur.

It is useful to locate contextual empiricism with regard to the arguments in Section 2, where I outlined the challenge to the Value Free Ideal from the AIR. Both Longino and Douglas think that non-epistemic values play a role in science because of underdetermination, but they focus on different kinds of underdetermination. For Douglas, the key problem is that our evidence under-determines our theory-choice; values are needed to decide *when* to make the leap to accept a theory. For Longino, the key problem is that it is not only the step from evidence to hypothesis that is underdetermined, but also the step from data to evidence; values are needed to interpret and shape what counts as evidence in the first place.[19] In Section 2, I outlined three responses to Douglas' inductive risk argument: to deny that it works; to accept that it works and say science cannot be objective; or to rethink the concept of objectivity. Although, as I just noted, Longino's account of the role of contextual values in reasoning focuses on a different form of underdetermination, it raises a similar challenge to objectivity. In turn, her response is a version of the third option: to rethink objectivity as requiring a form of critical community engagement; for know-ledge to be objective it must be made in a community organised in a particular sort of way. Plausibly, we might play a similar trick in response to the problems outlined in Section 2, then. Rather than try to refute the AIR, and its implication that all scientific justification is, ultimately, 'value-laden', we might, instead, welcome that conclusion, but reserve the term 'objective' for practices where inductive risk problems are solved by a process which involves broad commu-nity engagement. Indeed, some recent proposals in the literature on inductive risk suggest something similar; that scientists' response to inductive risk prob-lems should be guided by public preferences, rather than those of the individual scientist (Schroeder, 2017).

Even further back, in Section 1, I outlined the 'good old fashioned' notion of objectivity, construed as something like access to the world as it really is. Longino's work expresses a worry about the possibility of such representation; that our grip on the world is always mediated by certain sorts of assumptions which guide inference. However, she holds that this fact does not undermine the objectivity of our scientific products, as long as those assumptions have, themselves, been justified *via* a social procedure.

I have spent some time spelling out Longino's picture, both because it is widely influential and because it is a perfect exemplar of a wider strategy for grounding objectivity in social processes. Still, you might worry about various aspects of contextual empiricism. For example, the requirement that scientists engage with dissent may seem to ignore the benefits of dogmatism in science (Goldman, 2002); her proposals may seem to require that scientists engage with insincere manufactured dissent (Biddle and Leuschner, 2015); and there are obvious problems in deciding just whose views and values ought to be taken seriously in the first place (Hicks, 2011). In turn, various authors have clarified

---

[19] Of course, Douglas also thinks that inductive risk issues arise in the characterisation of evidence, as in the example of identifying tumours discussed in Section 2. Still, it seems that there is an important difference here insofar as Douglas' approach seems to assume that, at any point in the scientific process, we have evidence which allows us to assign a probability to a claim, and values are necessary to decide if those probabilities are 'high enough'. For Longino, by contrast, the concern is more that even the assignment of probabilities to hypotheses rests on a series of value-laden choices

and extended aspects of Longino's work to avoid these concerns (Wray, 1999; Borgerson, 2011).

Beyond these (important) debates about contextual empiricism, though, you might have a more fundamental concern that Longino's model itself is rather utopian; current scientific communities are far from the ideal, and it is hard to see how we might get them closer to it. However, although we may be far from Longino's ideal, her work can still be helpful as a way of thinking through various specific cases. As noted above, contextual empiricism provides a useful way of understanding the kind of criticism practised by scholars such as Lloyd. More generally, we can criticise *actual* practice by showing how far it deviates from the *ideal* conditions necessary for objectivity. (Consider, again, the analogy with Amartya Sen's work on justice: we might be able to identify some systems as unjust, even if we can't achieve full justice). For example, Jukola (2015) has argued that we can understand various apparent problems with current biomedical research in broadly contextual empiricist terms, focused on the ways in which value judgements are not open to community-wide debate and criticism. Note how this approach avoids some of the worries of accounting for concerns with industry-funded research in terms of the 'bias' discussed in the previous section. For Jukola, the problem is not that researchers make judgements, but that they make judgements in a manner which is not open for assessment and criticism by the community. (Although, conversely, research by Holman and Geislar (2018) suggest a twist to this tale, that institutional changes which may have seemed to make biomedical research closer to Longino's ideal were co-opted and corrupted by the pharmaceutical industry.) More generally, it is important to remember that objectivity is not necessarily *easy* to achieve or obtain. If Longino's work implies that we fall well short of full objectivity, this may be our problem, rather than a problem with her account of objectivity.

3.3 Bad Values and Good Science

Longino's work is often presented – both by herself and others – as stressing the *social* dimensions of scientific research. In some ways, this is peculiar. Imagine a fan of the product-centred notion of objectivity as the 'view from nowhere', briefly articulated in Section 1. Adherents of such a view are often accused of overlooking the fact that science is a social affair. This is rather an unfair criticism. A defender of good old-fashioned product objectivity might say that it is awfully difficult to achieve the view from nowhere, and that various social practices might make it far easier for us to overcome the relevant obstacles. For example, discussion with others might be an essential way of learning that what we thought were features of the world are, in fact, features of our own idiosyncratic way of representing the world. Something like this view might fit well with a notion, explored in Section 2, that social interactions can ensure that individual commitments and idiosyncratic biases are washed out through social processes. There is no reason why a proponent of traditional conceptions of objectivity – whether focused on products or processes – cannot help herself to the idea that social interactions are *important* aspects of inquiry.

The real problem, then, for standard views of objectivity is not that they are blind to the social dimensions of knowledge. Rather, the challenge they face is that, because of inductive risk concerns and/or the need for 'contextual values' in reasoning, we may simply be unable to 'remove' values from scientific justification *via* any procedure, individual or social. What, then, can we do? One option in response to this problem is to hold *if* we want a notion of objectivity, then we need an account of how to ensure that the values which structure science are, somehow, 'correct'. One way of understanding 'correct' here is relatively straightforward: we might think that certain values are just ethically or politically 'better' than others, such that science conducted according to the first set of values is 'better' than science conducted according to the second. Karen Intemann seems close to endorsing this view when she suggests that scientists should employ feminist values, rather than sexist or racist values (Intemann, 2011). Longino's approach, however, is more complex: scientific claims may inherently rest on values, but still be objective, just so long as the community is structured in such a way that those values have been, or could have been, debated, challenged and defended in various ways. For Longino, we cannot neatly divide contextual values up into a pile of 'good' and 'bad'; rather, what makes value-laden science objective is that the process whereby the values structure science is open and democratic. This is the sense in which her view introduces a new sense of the 'social': by making social discussion constitutive of objectivity, rather than just part of a larger process.

In turn, this approach fits well with various ways in which we use the language of objectivity. In treating truth and knowledge as the constitutive values of scientific inquiry, Longino links her account of objectivity to notions of representation (hence, meeting the 'fidelity' condition in Section 1); and, although her proposals may seem utopian, her work can guide practice (hence, meeting the 'viability' condition); finally, there is clearly something ethically and politically appealing in a model of free and equal exchange (hence, meeting the 'value' condition). Does this mean that we should happily throw our lot in with a model of objectivity centred around debate and criticism?

Unfortunately, case-studies are double-edged swords. To close this section, consider two such examples. Many standard histories of epidemiology date the discovery of the relationship between smoking and lung cancer to the work of two British epidemiologists, Richard Doll and Austin Bradford Hill, in the 1950s. However, the relationship was first established by German doctors writing in the 1920s and 1930s (Proctor, 2001). One reason this discovery is often airbrushed from history is that it was intimately related to Nazi political commitments, specifically a set of ideals of bodily purity and the importance of resisting foreign entry into this pure space. I take it for granted that the ethical and political values which structured these research projects are not the sorts of values which would stand up to critical scrutiny. Nonetheless, in this case at least, they seemed to allow researchers a better grasp on a real, important phenomenon. Of course, this is *not* to condone or support Nazi science specifically, or Nazi values more generally. Rather, it is to point to a very general problem: that it is not obvious that decent, acceptable ethical values are *necessary* for making epistemic progress. To make this point with a different example, Marx famously claimed that Darwin's theories were fundamentally shaped by his class position. Perhaps this claim is correct, in the sense that it was only because Darwin was committed to a particular worldview that he formulated his theories at all. Nonetheless, it is entirely possible that Darwin saw something *important* and *true*, even if we reject the worldview which led him to that insight (Lewens, 2016).

To put it bluntly, 'bad' values can be necessary or helpful for doing 'good' science. This phenomenon poses a serious challenge to saying that scientific objectivity requires that we employ the ethically 'correct' values; there are excellent ethical and political reasons to throw Nazis out of our community, but it is not clear that doing so improves our ability to do good science. Still, as we saw above, Longino does not think that good science requires that we employ ethically correct values, but only that the community is structured in such a way as to enable debate over values. Therefore, it seems that, in principle, Longino can avoid these concerns; for Longino, there is nothing wrong with Nazi values or cut-throat market values playing central roles in scientific theorising just as long as the process is structured such that those values are articulated, debated and defended. Indeed, you might think that the examples above imply that what Intemann treats as a problem for Longino – she leaves space for Nazis in the perfect scientific community! – is, in fact, a positive.

Still, I suggest we should be careful here, because Longino does seem to face a problem in specifying the scope of permissible criticism. Remember again that contextual values criss-cross the epistemic/non-epistemic divide: an androcentric bias in the study of the female orgasm looks problematic both on epistemic *and* on ethical or political grounds. This suggests an obvious question: in the process of debate, should we debate and criticise contextual values solely on 'epistemic' grounds or on both 'epistemic' and 'political' or 'ethical' grounds? The first approach seems incompatible with Longino's work, and the uses which others have made of it. More generally, it would seem very odd to undermine the distinction between epistemic/non-epistemic values and, yet, to think that, in actual debate, we should question those values using only epistemic concerns. The latter approach seems, then, closer to Longino's ideal, but now we face a second challenge: plausibly, Nazi scientists in an ideal contextual empiricist community can have their contextual values challenged on *ethical* grounds; in turn, if that community is well-ordered, they should be willing to take-up such criticisms, and change accordingly. Although Longino is careful not to claim that only the 'correct' values should structure science, her account of valid criticism and demand for uptake seems to face a similar problem: that it collapses the distinction between ethically acceptable values and epistemically trustworthy outcomes. This is problematic, because, as the case-studies above suggest, there seems to be a very straightforward sense in which 'bad' values can prompt good science.

At this point, you might be tempted to think that something odd is happening. When we try to articulate the relationship between objectivity, justification and values at a general or theoretical level, we end up in a giant mess: it seems both that justification *must* be value-laden and that non-epistemic values are *irrelevant* to justification! However, despite this theoretical mess, when we think about particular case-studies – say, research into the female orgasm, or the workings of the IPCC, or plate tectonics, or the link between smoking and lung cancer – we can figure out which pieces of research were reliable and trustworthy and which were not. We don't seem to *need* an account of objectivity: why not just give up on the concept altogether?

4 Is Objectivity Just Male Subjectivity?

At the very start of this discussion, I noted that nearly every article or book on the topic of objectivity starts by noting the variety of ways the term is used: Douglas suggests eight dimensions; Janack trumps her with 13; and so on. Faced with this philosophical thicket, one option is to try to find, or impose, some common core or common thread of meaning. That is what I have done so far. Another option, however, is to suggest we should give up on the concept of objectivity entirely. Thinking about these proposals requires us to ask what purposes are served by talk of objectivity. One answer, often associated with standpoint epistemologies, points to the ways in which concepts of objectivity can serve as tools of subordination and domination. This section is devoted to exploring this negative or debunking approach, which, on the face of it, may seem good grounds for eliminating the concept altogether. However, there is a twist; one of the key proponents of standpoint theory, Sandra Harding, has proposed an account of objectivity which is surprisingly close to good old-fashioned product-centred accounts of objectivity, as exemplified by Robert Nozick's account of objectivity as invariance. In conclusion, then, I will explore some of these resonances, and their more general implications for the task of constructing a usable notion of scientific objectivity from the wreckage of Sections 2 and 3.

4.1 Against Objectivity

In the recent literature, two prominent philosophers have promoted the idea of giving up the concept of objectivity altogether.

First, Ian Hacking (2015) has suggested that objectivity talk is useless. Hacking's concern is based on two points: first, that objectivity is primarily 'negative', in the sense that the concept points to an *absence* of (certain kinds of) influence on a process, rather than *positive* epistemic virtues; and, second, that it functions as an 'elevator word', taking us away from the nitty-gritty details of practice to an abstraction. Hacking suggests that if we actually want to convince people to *trust* the results of some process, saying that the process is 'objective' does not work. Rather, we need to point to positive, first-order features of that methodology; features that the process possesses, rather than features it lacks.

The second attack has been launched by Matthew Brown (2019). Brown worries that the concept of objectivity is connected with the 'Value Free Ideal'. In turn, he holds that various arguments – including, but not only, those summarised in Sections 2 and 3 – show that this Ideal is unsustainable. Brown concedes that various authors have tried to create accounts of objectivity which recognise that inference might be value-laden. However, he suggests that such accounts bundle together disparate epistemic virtues. Furthermore, even if they are successful on their own terms, the concept of objectivity will invariably be understood by broader audiences as implying that social and political values are distortions of good science. On his account, then, attempts to redefine objectivity perpetuate confused images of science, with bad social and political consequences.

In short, for Hacking and Brown, we do not *need* a concept of objectivity, in the sense that the concept adds nothing to debate, and we are *better-off*, both conceptually and politically, jettisoning such talk. If you have made it so far in this Element, you may have similar concerns. I will return to consider concerns about the emptiness of the concept of objectivity later. For current purposes, however, it is useful to focus in on Brown's more political concerns: that objectivity talk diverts our attention from the inevitable involvement of non-epistemic values in science, distorting public debate. Brown's worries point to a more general fault line in debates over objectivity. As I noted in Section 1, debates over whether we can and do achieve objectivity are intimately related to broader political debates. For some, attacks on the concept of objectivity are part of a broader attack on the institutions of liberal democracy. For others, overthrowing the concept of objectivity is part of a more general liberatory struggle, premised on the idea that claims about objectivity are tools for perpetuating problematic forms of political and social hegemony. As an example of the latter approach, consider Adrienne Rich's striking aphorism that 'objectivity is male subjectivity'. On the face of it, this slogan suggests that the very concept of objectivity functions as a way of denying women's voices.

Note, however, an ambiguity in political concerns about objectivity. No-one could sensibly deny that claims about objectivity *have*, as a matter of fact, often functioned as tools of unjust social and political exclusion. Does that mean, though, that we should give up on objectivity, or just that we need a better account of true objectivity? Many recent debates over objectivity stem from broadly Marxist concerns. However, classical Marxist thought had a complex account of objectivity (Railton, 1984). For the Marxist, ideology leads the bourgeois theorist to mistake contingent features of the ownership of the means of production as reflecting necessary, unchanging features of the world. Claims about what is 'objectively' true *do* function as ways of perpetuating a political-economic structure. However, classical Marxists did not claim that we must, therefore, give up on a notion of objectivity, because the promise of Marxist theory was supposed to be precisely that it provided a *properly* objective account of the workings of society, undistorted by the lens of class interest. The bourgeois theorist's problem is not that she thinks that objectivity is *possible* or *desirable*, but, rather, that, in virtue of her class position, she is *wrong* about what is objective. It is possible, then, both to think that actual claims to objectivity are problematic – for example, they are just reifications of male subjectivity – while holding oneself to have the properly objective picture. In turn, presumably this perspective is valuable and important precisely because it tells us what the world is *really* like. Indeed, as we have noted, many leading feminist scholars, such as Longino, are keen to 'reclaim' objectivity (see Janack, 2002, for a very helpful overview). In short, the politics of objectivity is trickier than it may at first appear.

4.2 Harding and Standpoint Theory

Many contemporary concerns about the politics of objectivity stem from 'standpoint epistemologies'. In this section, then, I will set out the views of one leading standpoint theorist, Sandra Harding, and, specifically, her complex account of objectivity.

One easy way into the core concepts of standpoint epistemology is *via* the related concept of a perspective. If you have climbed a tree and I am at the bottom of the tree, we will be in a position to know very different things about the landscape; you can see the cows in the distance, whereas I can see the ant crawling on the ground. We can understand standpoint epistemology as generalising the concept of a physical perspective to a wider, social sense. Certain sorts of knowledge, or knowledge of certain (kinds of) facts, can only or best be apprehended from individuals in particular, historically and culturally situated social positions (Harding, 2015, chapter 1).[20] Specifically, standpoint theorists often stress a claim related to the classical Marxist concern about the effects of ideology; that those in positions of subordination may be particularly well-placed to have forms of knowledge which are not accessible to those in socially 'superior' situations. In turn, these forms of knowledge tend to be downplayed or ignored by those in dominant social situations. For the standpoint theorist, then, it is important to recognise that social order and epistemic systems are 'co-produced'; how we research (and how we think we ought to research) is intimately related to notions of how we organise (and how we think we ought to organise) society (Harding, 2015, chapter 1).

Unsurprisingly, standpoint epistemology is often closely allied with feminist and post-colonial movements which stress the ways in which socially and politically marginalised groups – women, the colonised, people of colour – have also suffered from epistemic marginalisation. One of Harding's interesting examples concerns the navigational skills and knowledge of Micronesian Islanders (Harding, 2015, chapter 4). She suggests that, although such indigenous knowledge 'mostly . . . produces reliable knowledge and is fair to data and critical perspectives' (Harding, 2015, 8), it is typically systematically dismissed by White colonialists, as backward superstition, hence legitimating colonial interventions in the name of improvement. In such examples, there is an important link between standpoint epistemology and notions of epistemic injustice: that is, cases where stereotypes and biases lead members of certain groups to suffer 'credibility deficits', where their genuine knowledge is ignored or downgraded (Fricker, 2007).

---

[20] Note that I focus here on Harding's most recent work (Harding 2015), but interested readers should also consult earlier work, especially Harding, 1991 and Wylie, 2003

Before going on, it is worth noting a general difficulty in assessing and explaining standpoint theory. On the one hand, standpoint theories can sometimes seem like little more than extended common sense. Of course, the person up a tree can see things that someone at the bottom cannot; by analogy, of course the person who has suffered oppression has knowledge of what it is like to suffer oppression which her oppressor may lack. On the other hand, standpoint theories can sometimes seem highly revisionary; as if our socio-cultural background means that we live in radically different worlds, each with its own epistemic rules. The first reading threatens to render standpoint theory uninteresting – it is merely a reminder that different people can have different experiences – but the second reading threatens to render it incoherent – why respect the knowledge of different social groups if that is merely 'their' knowledge? One way of constructing a position in-between these extremes is by distinguishing between different *ways* of gaining knowledge. For the standpoint theorist, group membership shapes knowledge acquisition in a deep way, such that, for certain kinds of knowledge *only* members of some group, enculturated in particular ways, can gain or access that knowledge through experience. In this sense, standpoints are unlike, say, the vantage point from up-the-tree, which is, in principle, open to anyone. However, this knowledge can be articulated and offered in testimony. In turn, then, we should be receptive to the testimony of members of other groups, even when their claims seem odd or unusual from our perspective. We are not necessarily sealed into hermetic epistemic bubbles.

To think through standpoint epistemology, and, in particular, its relationship to objectivity, it is useful to have an example. Typically, Harding and other standpoint theorists focus on issues around gender, race and colonialism. However, to help illustrate the breadth and range of the theory, I will explore an example centred around social class, based on work by the sociologist Brian Wynne (1996). (It is worth noting that Wynne himself does not explicitly frame his work in standpoint theory terms but the overlap of interests is striking.) After the accident at the Chernobyl nuclear reactor in 1986, there were worries that radioactive fallout might affect Cumbria in the North East of England. Specifically, scientists were concerned that sheep might graze on affected grass, and, hence, that radioactive material would enter the human food chain. As a result, a group of scientists were sent to Cumbria to explore the degree of radiation and to advise farmers and local government officials on how best to handle the risk of contamination. At this point, I recommend reading Wynne's work account of how the official scientists ended up ignoring and overlooking the situated knowledge of the sheep farmers. If it were not for the vast costs involved, Wynne's story would be almost comic in the forms of official ineptitude it portrays. For example, government scientists closely studied areas where sheep never grazed, desperately chased sheep around farmyards waving Geiger counters and ignored reports on how local livestock markets worked. The result of this deep scientific ignorance of local conditions, misapplication of general models and faulty measurement led to a series of recommendations that had little to no relationship to the realities or possibilities on the ground. In this case, it seems clear that far better and more effective advice would have been developed had the scientists not been so wedded to their general theories and models, but, instead, listened to the farmers' local, situated knowledge.

At a first glance, Wynne's study may seem interesting and important, but relatively straightforward: of course, if you want to know about *local* sheep grazing patterns, you should listen to *local* farmers! Importantly, however, Wynne suggests that this apparent failure involved more than a failure to listen to the farmers' specific factual claims – say, about how sheep *actually* grazed, as opposed to how the models *said* they grazed – but a more general clash of different styles or types of knowledge. In virtue of their training and social background, the scientists thought of the natural world in essentially mechanistic, calculable terms, whereas, in virtue of their experience, the farmers were more attuned to the holistic interplay of different factors. For Wynne, the difference between scientists and farmers is not simply that the farmers were aware of facts which the scientists missed, but that the two groups had different *ways* of knowing about the world. In turn, the scientists would have done better work – in the sense that they would have derived a more accurate picture of the world and made more sensible proposals – had they deferred to the kinds of claims generated by the farmers' form of knowledge, rather than rejecting it as unscientific.

Of course, specific case-studies are always contestable. Nonetheless, examples such as Wynne's illustrate a more general phenomenon: that there can be a clash between the forms of knowledge and understanding possessed by scientific experts and the knowledge and understanding of other groups, where it is very unclear that the former is necessarily 'better', in the sense of more accurate or more helpful, than the latter. Plausibly, many social policies would be far better – in the purely instrumental sense of achieving their explicit goals – were they more attuned to forms of inquiry and knowledge that do not fit well within contemporary scientific norms. However, it is precisely these scientific norms and standards that we typically associate with 'objectivity'. As Harding suggests (Harding, 2015, chapter 1), there are strong links between notions of Modernisation, as applied in development economics to 'improve' the Global South and notions of objectivity, rationality and research methods. In Cumbria, the scientists measured and calculated in an 'objective' way, whereas the farmers seemed to rely on a complex, uncodified combination of experience and intuition. Therefore, following a broadly standpoint epistemology approach, we might be tempted to follow Brown's 'anti-objectivity' line: valorising objectivity forecloses epistemically valuable avenues of inquiry in ways that perpetuate existing political and economic inequalities.

Interestingly, however, Harding does not reject objectivity talk (Harding, 2015, chapter 2). Rather, she draws a distinction between what she calls 'weak' and 'strong' objectivity. A claim is 'weakly' objective if it counts as objective given the methods and tools available within some particular social-epistemic framework. For example, maybe the scientists' claims about the likely degree of radioactive contamination were 'weakly' objective given the norms for establishing radioactivity. A claim is 'strongly' objective, by contrast, when it is well-established from each-and-every standpoint. To take a trivial example, the fact that sheep graze is one which could be agreed upon both by the scientists and the sheep farmers, and, as such, is a 'strongly objective' fact (albeit, a dull one). More seriously, we might think that, had the scientists taken more heed of the farmers' concerns, then their recommendations might have been based on claims which were 'strongly' objective; that is, which counted as well-established from both sets of perspectives. In turn, Harding thinks that only 'strong objectivity' captures the shared core meaning of the language of objectivity: that objective research is 'fair to the evidence, fair to its critics, and fair to the most severe criticisms' (Harding, 2015, 33). Weak objectivity fails to meet this ideal, insofar as it limits itself to responding to criticisms which arise *within* some community, rather than those which arise from *other* socially situated standpoints.

Note that Harding does not think that *only* strongly objective knowledge is important, or even that strongly objective claims are better than or preferable to weakly objective claims. After all, the key aim of standpoint epistemology is precisely to get us to take 'situated' knowledge seriously. However, strongly objective knowledge is important, because it is only when claims are strongly objective that we can be assured that acting on those claims will not impose our epistemic and political norms upon others. The notion of being 'fair' to evidence and criticisms is telling here, insofar as the concept is ambiguous between an epistemic and an ethical sense. In terms of our feminist slogan above, Harding agrees that we often mistakenly conflate 'male subjectivity' with 'objectivity'. However, this does not show that the concept of objectivity is unimportant. Rather, it is an instance of being confused about what is truly, strongly objective.

Harding's theory may seem closely related to Longino's contextual empiricism. However, although both theories grow out of feminist epistemology and its insights into how knowledge might be shaped by identities and interests, they differ in important respects. Longino's approach holds that the values which shape knowledge production must have been tested in critical debate for the resulting epistemic products to be objective; objective knowledge requires a procedure where embedded value commitments are assessed (or assessable) by all. For Harding, by contrast, there is no demand that communities open themselves up to criticism by other communities. (Indeed, such criticism might itself be a site of the kinds of silencing and injustice which worry her.) Rather, in principle at least, different groups might employ radically different values to generate claims. Whether claims are 'strongly objective' is a function of whether members of the different communities can, or do, agree on the conclusions of inquiry.

In Section 1, I outlined one key move in recent work on objectivity, away from a focus on whether epistemic products represent the world as it really is, shorn of human influence, and towards a focus on questions of trustworthiness. In turn, I argued that this shift is related to a move away from thinking about objectivity as a feature of the *products* of inquiry to a focus on objectivity as a feature of the *processes* which generate epistemic products. Harding's suggestions relate to these moves in an interesting way: she moves the focus of objectivity talk back to products, rather than processes.[21] This is the fundamental difference between her approach and Longino's approach, which seeks to secure objectivity in knowledge claims being generated through a particular kind of social interaction. (Indeed, Harding herself suggests that she differs from other feminist philosophers of science in that she starts from the reality of the world and oppression (Harding, 2015, 31). I don't think this is a fair criticism, but it certainly suggests a deep suspicion of the notion that we should focus on processes, rather than material realties.) However, Harding is also keen to stress that claims might not be strongly objective, but should still be trusted. That is to say, she stresses that objectivity is *sufficient*, rather than *necessary*, for trustworthiness. How should we think of this move, and how does it relate to proposals to do away with objectivity talk altogether?

---

[21] Note an oddity here. In her list of different senses of objectivity, Douglas talks about what she calls 'convergent objectivity', where 'we approach the result through multiple avenues, and if the same result continues to appear, we have increasing confidence in the reliability of the result' (Douglas, 2004, 457). Obviously, 'convergent objectivity' looks a lot like 'strong objectivity', but Douglas says that convergent objectivity is a form of *process* objectivity, whereas I say 'strong objectivity' is about *products*. In this case, I think that Douglas' characterisation is just wrong: when a claim is justified through multiple processes (or *via* different avenues or from different standpoints), it is the *fact* of convergence which gives us reason to trust the *product*; whether we actively went through a process of seeking convergence is a separate question, irrelevant to assessment of the objectivity of the product

4.3 Strong Objectivity as Strongly Objective: From Harding to Nozick

If, like me, you have realist inclinations, you might worry that there is something troubling about Harding's definition of strong objectivity: there is a difference between a claim being widely agreed upon and that claim being true. I will return to this worry shortly. First, however, I want to explore some overlaps between Harding's work and other approaches to the topic of objectivity.

First, consider Anna Alexandrova's work on what she calls 'mixed claims'; for example, economists' claims that increases in income do not cause improvements in well-being or epidemiologists' claims that stress causes ill-health. (Alexandrova, 2017, chapter 4). Plausibly, such claims can be better or worse supported by available evidence, and we can judge whether scientists have allowed their own commitments to affect their conclusions. For example, we might worry that an epidemiologist whose reputation rests on showing that stress is an important risk factor for disease is not able to assess evidence for this claim. In this way, mixed claims look like the kinds of claims which we can, quite straightforwardly, talk of as more or less 'objective', in the simple process sense outlined in Section 2. However, 'mixed claims' differ from other causal or statistical claims in that at least one key variable is defined in ways which presuppose a moral, prudential or political value judgement; terms such as 'well-being' or 'health' implicitly presuppose value judgements concerning what counts as a 'good' life or 'normal' functioning. As we noted in Section 2, there is a strong sense that value judgements are antithetical to objectivity. So, quite apart from all of the issues we raised in Sections 2 and 3 about values in inference, 'mixed claims' pose an interesting problem about the extent to which scientific claims can both be objective *and* value-laden.

To address these worries, Alexandrova starts by identifying two, related concerns about mixed claims: first, a concern about 'inattention' (that we might use controversial, value-laden terms without recognising we are doing so); which leads to a risk of 'imposition' (that using these terms might lead us to overlook or deny or override others' values) (Alexandrova, 2017, 93–94). For Alexandrova, unless we are attentive to these concerns, our scientific practices risk becoming a form of 'coercive paternalism'. To counter these concerns, she suggests that when scientists use mixed claims, they should follow a three-step process: they should (1) make value presuppositions explicit; (2) check presuppositions for controversy; and (3) when controversial, consult relevant parties. According to Alexandrova, following this process helps scientists ensure that any 'mixed claims' they make can be 'objective', even when those claims presuppose distinctively ethical value judgements (Alexandrova, 2017, chapter 4).

Although not grounded in a standpoint epistemology, Alexandrova's strategy for securing objectivity is interestingly similar to Harding's project. The language of 'inattention' and 'imposition' provides a nice way of capturing some of Harding's concerns about the dangers of conflating 'weak' and 'strong' objectivity. In turn, we can think of Alexandrova's proposals as a way of securing strong, rather than weak, objectivity for mixed claims. Through consultation, we ensure that, even if mixed claims do involve some value-laden concepts, those concepts can be endorsed from multiple (relevant) standpoints, rather than merely one standpoint. Of course, there are important differences between Harding and Alexandrova; most notably, Alexandrova is far closer to a process-centred than product-centred view. However, it is striking how both use notions of agreement across different perspectives to spell out a notion of objectivity in response to concerns about the imposition of values.

Even more striking is the resonance between Harding's strong objectivity and the work of Robert Nozick (2001). Nozick – a philosopher whose political views differ from Harding's greatly – proposes an account of objectivity in terms of 'invariance under admissible transformations'. To get a grasp on this concept, Nozick suggests that some feature of the environment which is perceived in both human and cricket observation is psychologically 'more objective' than something which only humans can observe. In turn, he explicitly links this concept of objectivity with the philosophy of physics, mirroring Paul Dirac's claim that the 'important things in the world are invariant under Lorentz transformations'. On the face of it, then, Nozick might seem to be working in the tradition of Nagel and Williams, where 'objectivity' concerns the ultimate constituents of reality. Indeed, Nozick himself is clear that his task is primarily to understand such canonical topics as the basis of intersubjective agreement or the nature of objective knowledge.

However, as it turns out, Nozick's account of objectivity allows for a large degree of contextualisation. For example, he is happy to speak of historical claims as being objective when they can be agreed upon regardless of historians' own theoretical perspectives or political allegiances (even if, presumably, insects would have to opinion on the causes of the French Revolution). In effect, Nozick's talk of Lorentz transformations is a metaphor for establishing a notion of objective claims as claims whose truth or acceptability does not vary with the perspective of particular (communities of) inquirers. It is easy to see that this notion of invariance maps nicely into Harding's strong objectivity; for Nozick, objectivity is secured only when those adopting very different standpoints on some phenomenon come to the same conclusions. Furthermore, Nozick is at pains to stress that his conception of objectivity is in line with value judgements playing an essential role in scientific work, suggesting that the use of 'non-objective' value judgements in science need not 'contaminate' the products of inquiry (Nozick, 2001, 95). Finally, Nozick concedes much to what, following Harding, we might call the claims of weak objectivity, stressing that, for many practical purposes, claims which are variant may be 'good enough' for practical action. In short, although his arguments are part of a very different philosophical and political project, Nozick's account of objectivity as invariance shares striking similarities with Harding's project.

Although they start from radically different positions – a concern with the political-epistemic legacies of colonialism; a concern with value-presuppositions in the social sciences; a concern with traditional metaphysical worries – there is a striking convergence between Harding, Alexandrova and Nozick on objectivity as invariance. It is tempting to use this convergence to argue for an account of objective as invariance – but, unfortunately, that would be a circular argument. (Although its intuitive appeal is, perhaps, telling.) Beyond this convergence, then, why think of objectivity in terms of invariance? To address this question, remember the three conditions on an account of objectivity sketched in Section 1: that it should have fidelity with our everyday uses of the term as linked to accurate representation, it should pick out something valuable and it should be viable.

The concept of objectivity as invariance is faithful to some aspects of our everyday objectivity talk. An important aspect of objectivity is that it is opposed to idiosyncrasy; we can understand invariant claims as those which are considered true, regardless of our particular standpoint, and, in that sense, as non-idiosyncratic. Note that, because notions of strong objectivity or objectivity-as-invariance focus on *products*, they do not capture the sense that objectivity is related to following particular *processes*. Still, as we have seen from Sections 2 and 3, identifying a plausible account of which processes promote objectivity is no easy task – maybe this is a strength, rather than a weakness.

On *viability*, matters are more complex. Plausibly, we may never know whether a claim is established from *every* standpoint or invariant under *every* transformation. Still, we can get some way towards assessing whether claims meet the invariance condition by testing how they fare relative to actual existing frameworks or standpoints. In this way, notions of invariance or strong objectivity are more grounded than a 'view from nowhere'. There is a genuine mystery as to how we might ever know whether we were *really* viewing things from nowhere. By contrast, we have some sense of how we might check whether different frameworks do agree. The more serious challenge, perhaps, is in distinguishing between good and bad forms of (apparent) agreement. After all, it is not hard to get people to *say* that they agree with your claims, even when they don't, especially when they are disempowered or marginalised.

Finally, why think that invariance or strong objectivity is valuable? There are several possible responses to this challenge. First, there is a broadly realist argument that agreement on some claim from different perspectives is a good reason (perhaps the best reason) to think this claim represents the world accurately. If we want our beliefs to track the truth, we have particularly good reason to pay attention to invariant or objective claims. Second, we might adopt a broadly pragmatist stance, and suggest whether it is meaningless to ask whether a claim which is invariant under transformations or justifiable from every standpoint is *really* true; by definition, it is the best we can get! Third, there is an ethical or political argument, offered by both Harding and Alexandrova, that in using invariant claims we do not risk imposing *our* values on others. To think about this idea, remember Betz's concern about the AIR: if scientific justification is value-laden, it seems that when we make factual claims to others, we (implicitly) impose our values upon them (Betz, 2013). Betz's own response to this concern is to try to drain justification of values. Notions of strong objectivity reflect a different response: to identify claims which, some-how, cohere with *everyone's* values (John, 2019).

Brown worries that the concept of objectivity necessarily implies that justifi-cation is 'value-free', and, hence, is politically dangerous; objectivity as invari-ance avoids these charges. Contrary to Hacking's concerns, the concept of invariance does not simply equate objectivity with various *absences* from scientific process, but, rather, points to a useful way of spelling out a difference between different kinds of knowledge claims. Like Longino's account of objectivity, the invariance approach notes the importance of recog-nising a multiplicity of voices but avoids collapsing the distinction between politically acceptable and epistemically valuable commitments. Finally, a focus on invariance neatly captures the notion that objectivity is closely related to notions of trust – what, after all, could be *more* trustworthy than a claim which can be established from *every* standpoint?

Note that none of this is to say that an account of strong objectivity or objectivity as invariance is straightforward or simple. For example, scientific change often involves challenges to standard or dominant positions; claims which seem, in some sense, 'shared' from all perspectives. Presumably, we do not want to say that such scientists are failing to be objective; rather, they are suggesting that there is a difference between a claim *seeming* to be established from each standpoint and it *actually being* established. This is an intuitive distinction, but hard to spell out. This specific problem points to a far more general issue around notions of objectivity in terms of invariance, that they face a challenge around inclusion and exclusion. It seems plausible that some frameworks or approaches to thinking about the world are completely confused or plain wrong. For example, even the most epistemically liberal philosopher might think that frameworks for social or historical explanation framed in terms of massive shadowy conspiracies directed by aliens can safely be ignored. If every single sociological framework other than the 'massive alien conspiracy framework' agrees on some claim about the world, that seems enough to treat the claim as objectively true. However, spelling out this thought is tricky, because we seem to require some account of when frameworks are worth taking seriously and when they are not. Precisely the key lesson of standpoint epistemology is that we may be atrociously bad at this task because our judgements may be guided or shaped by all sorts of irrelevant or pernicious factors. Operationalising invariance is no simple task.

4.4 The New Wave

In Section 1, I noted the fall of the good old-fashioned view of objectivity in terms of a 'view from nowhere' in favour of a focus on procedures. One result of this shift was a growing awareness among philosophers of science of the sheer range and breadth of the ways in which we use the term 'objectivity'. At the same time, there was a growing move in philosophy of science away from singular accounts of *the* scientific method, towards a recognition of the many different ways in which different disciplines explore the world (Fine, 1998). In addition, accounts of objectivity were further complicated by the trends we noted in Sections 2 and 3, towards recognising the role of values in justification. As a result, conceptions of objectivity have multiplied and complexified over the last 40 years.

One response to such complexity is to embrace it and work with it, as in Douglas' claim that the concept of objectivity is 'irreducibly complex', with myriad senses only loosely collected under some vague notion of trustworthiness (Douglas, 2004). Another option, outlined at the start of this section is to argue that we do not need the concept at all, and simply eliminate it. It is, after all, hard to see how objectivity talk can help us in our day-to-day task of placing and withholding trust if that concept is, itself, so complex. A third option is to try to seek some unity to the concept of objectivity beyond the thin notion of trustworthiness. Above, I set out one such approach, suggesting a sense of objectivity in terms of invariance. However, other approaches are available. To conclude, then, in the spirit of pluralistic debate, I shall outline two recent, interesting proposals for reconceptualising objectivity, both of which remain focused more closely on *processes*, rather than *products*: from Jack Wright (2018) and from Inkeri Koskinen (2018).

Both Wright and Koskinen start from the claim that the concept of objectivity is essentially contextual, in the sense that what counts as 'objective' methods of inquiry may differ across different disciplines. Techniques that ensure objectivity in some scientific discipline may not be necessary for objectivity in a second discipline. Nonetheless, they both claim that this form of contextualism is compatible with objectivity having a more precise and specific meaning than merely serving as a synonym for 'trustworthy'.

For Wright, objectivity talk always involves what he calls 'taking a step back'. To use some of his own examples, when a central bank claims to have an 'objective' view of the economy, this claim should be interpreted as meaning that its view is one which is at a step removed from the 'everyday' perspective of consumers or politicians. In this sense, then, Wright captures part of the appeal of the notion of objectivity as involving a 'view from nowhere' without endorsing the (metaphysically and epistemologically puzzling) claim that there *is* a (humanly accessible) view from nowhere to be had. Whereas Nagel holds that the process of stepping back is a starting point which can be 'repeated, yielding a still more objective conception' (Nagel, 1986, 4), Wright is happy to stop way before the familiar world disappears. Rather, Wright stresses that notions of objectivity are linked to our purposes; being objective requires that we step as far back as is necessary to achieve our goals in the best manner. A central bank needs to step back far enough to achieve its goals; in doing so, it achieves objectivity, even if, on a further step back, 'money' or 'inflation' would simply disappear from our view altogether.

Koskinen (2018), by contrast, is more interested in explaining the variation in our use of the language of objectivity. Her proposal starts from the concept of 'epistemic risks'. As she uses this term, epistemic risks are factors that threaten our ability to make accurate or true claims about the world. For example, we might understand cognitive biases, or pressures from funding bodies, or political pressures as sources of epistemic risks. Epistemic trust requires some assurance that investigators have taken steps to reduce or mitigate these epistemic risks. (Note that Koskinen stresses what she calls *reliance* rather than *trust*: see my comments in Section 1.) For Koskinen, objectivity can be accounted for in terms of such trust: to say that some set of epistemic methods or techniques is objective is to say that those methods or techniques are such as to reduce or mitigate certain sorts of epistemic risks; to say that a research community is objective is to say that various collective biases are averted. A nice feature of Koskinen's account is that she clarifies that objectivity concerns epistemic risks stemming from our imperfections as epistemic agents, rather than all epistemic challenges. For example, the fact that the world is recalcitrant to our investigations is not itself the kind of epistemic risk which undermines objective science, whereas, by contrast, cognitive biases are. In making this clarification, she provides a fascinating account of the subtly moralised features of our talk of objectivity, as related to our own failings.

Importantly, however, different kinds of epistemic risks might be most salient or problematic for different kinds of investigations into different kinds of phenomena. For example, in doing medical research, funding bias might be an important source of epistemic risk, whereas in doing sociological research, a refusal to listen to participants' experiences might be a significant source of epistemic risk. Hence, the methods and techniques needed to ensure objectivity in medical science may be very different from the methods and techniques needed to ensure objectivity in sociological research. More generally, Koskinen hopes to incorporate the concerns of Harding and other standpoint epistemologists, by suggesting that exclusion of various epistemic perspectives is, often, epistemically risky (although, of course, over-inclusion can carry its own risks as well). For Koskinen, many arguments about objectivity are, then, best understood as arguments about which epistemic risks are most important to mitigate or avoid in some context. As a result, the concept of objectivity *is* complex, and we should not try to impose a one-size-fits-all model *across* the sciences. However, this complexity is not, as Douglas (2004) would have it, *irreducible*: at a higher-level, our objectivity talk is united by a concern to minimise epistemic risk.

Wright's approach and Koskinen's approach differ in important regards. This Element is not the place to pursue those debates. Rather, I want to stress the important similarities between their work: a trend in philosophy of science towards finding accounts of objectivity which are sensitive to variation between different epistemic enterprises and contexts of inquiry, but which go beyond equating objectivity with trustworthy. In turn, both provide excellent arguments against some of the concerns discussed at the start of this section. Wright suggests that Hacking's broadly pragmatist concern that objectivity talk always involves moving away from practice to an abstraction is misguided, because abstractions can be useful for guiding first-order reasoning, by helping us see the links between familiar and unfamiliar cases. Similarly, Koskinen suggests that the negative nature of objectivity claims need not be a worry, because controlling epistemic risks simply is a key part of ensuring that scientific work is trustworthy.

4.5 Recap

At the start of this section, I outlined some important challenges to objectivity talk. These challenges focus on the utility – or otherwise – of objectivity talk.

How can it help, if at all, in the day-to-day hurly-burly of epistemic to-and-fro? Does the concept of 'objectivity' get in the way of articulating and pursuing socially, politically and ethically important goals? If so, does this suggest that *our* concept of objectivity is faulty or that the concept *itself* should be replaced? These challenges are not made in ignorance of the complex ways in which philosophers of science have reconfigured accounts of objectivity over the last few decades. Rather, they are worries prompted by those accounts and the complexities they have introduced. In this section, I have considered responses to these challenges, and, of course, many more – including versions of accounts discussed earlier in this volume – are available. Still, I cannot claim to have shown that Hacking's and Brown's concerns can be met.

Nor would I want to claim that. There are very many interesting and important questions about the proper role of broadly non-epistemic values in science – must scientists appeal to non-epistemic values? If they must, how ought they do so? How do concerns about 'values' in science relate to notions of trust? – and how these relate to claims that we ought to trust scientists. It is unclear that a term as slippery and complex as 'objectivity' can helpfully resolve all of these kinds of questions. However, it remains extremely important to ask how we do, might and should use the concept of objectivity. Partly, this is for intellectual reasons; precisely because concepts of objectivity are so widely discussed across philosophy of science, thinking through this term is a helpful way of thinking about a wide range of different debates and how they relate. It is also, though, for practical reasons. I understand the urge which leads Hacking and Brown to suggest that we should jettison 'objectivity' talk entirely from our philosophical vocabulary. However, philosophers cannot legislate away the fact that the term circulates in and structures a wide range of public debates over the place of science in society and of society in science. Whatever we say in journal articles or books, the rest of the world will continue to treat objectivity as important. If philosophy is to be helpful, then, it would be good to have something to say about which processes and products should get the accolade of being objective.

References

Alexandrova, A. (2017) *A Philosophy for the Science of Well Being*. New York, NY: Oxford University Press

Anderson, E. (2004) 'Uses of value judgments in science: A general argument, with lessons from a case study of feminist research on divorce'. *Hypatia, 19*(1), 1–24

Axtell, G. (2015) *Objectivity*. Cambridge: Polity Press

Badano, G., John, S., & Junghans, T. (2017) 'NICE's Cost-Effectiveness Threshold' in McClimans, L. (ed) *Measurement in Medicine: Philosophical Essays on Assessment and Evaluation*. London: Rowman and Littlefield

Bertolaso, M., & Sterpetti, F. (2019) 'Evidence amalgamation, plausibility, and cancer research'. *Synthese, 196*(8), 3279–3317

Betz, G. (2013) 'In defence of the value free ideal'. *European Journal for Philosophy of Science, 3*(2), 207–220

Biddle, J. B., & Leuschner, A. (2015) 'Climate skepticism and the manufacture of doubt: can dissent in science be epistemically detrimental?' *European Journal for Philosophy of Science, 5*(3), 261–278

Biddle, J. B., & Kukla, R. (2017) 'The geography of epistemic risk' in Elliott, K., ed. *Exploring Inductive Risk: Case Studies of Values in Science*. Oxford: Oxford University Press, pp. 215–238

Bird, A. (2019) 'Systematicity, knowledge, and bias. How systematicity made clinical medicine a science'. *Synthese, 196*(3), 863–879

Bolinska, A. (2013) 'Epistemic representation, informativeness and the aim of faithful representation'. *Synthese, 190*(2), 219–234

Borgerson, K. (2011) 'Amending and defending critical contextual empiricism'. *European Journal for Philosophy of Science, 1*(3), 435

Bowcott, O. (2019) 'Judge rules against researcher who lost job over trans-gender tweets'. *The Guardian* 18 Dec 2019 www.theguardian.com/society/2019/dec/18/judge-rules-against-charity-worker-who-lost-job-over-trans gender-tweets

Brown, M. J. (2019) 'Is science really value free and objective?' in McKain, K. and Kampouaris, K. (eds) *What is Scientific Knowledge?: An Introduction to Contemporary Epistemology of Science*. London: Routledge

Churchman, C. (1948) 'Statistics, Pragmatics, Induction'. *Philosophy of Science, 15*, 249–268

Culp, S. (1995). 'Objectivity in experimental inquiry: breaking data-technique circles'. *Philosophy of Science, 62*(3), 438–458

Daston, L. and Galison, P. (2007) *Objectivity*. Cambridge, MA: MIT Press

Douglas, H. (2000) 'Inductive risk and values in science'. *Philosophy of Science*, *67*(4), 559–579

Douglas, H. (2004) 'The irreducible complexity of objectivity'. *Synthese*, *138*(3), 453–473

Douglas, H. (2009) *Science, Policy and the Value-Free Ideal*. Pittsburgh, PA: University of Pittsburgh Press

Fine, A.I. (1984) 'The Natural Ontological Attitude', in Leplin, J., (ed.), *Scientific Realism*. University of California Press, pp. 261–277.

Fine, A. (1998) 'The viewpoint of no-one in particular'. *Proceedings and Addresses of the American Philosophical Association*, *72*(2),7–20

Fricker, M. (2007) *Epistemic Injustice*. Oxford: Oxford University Press

Gaukroger, S. (2012) *Objectivity: A Very Short Introduction*. Oxford: Oxford University Press

Gigerenzer, G., & Selten, R. (Eds). (2002). *Bounded Rationality: The Adaptive Toolbox*. Cambridge, MA: MIT Press

Goldman, A. I. (2001) 'Experts: Which ones should you trust?' *Philosophy and Phenomenological Research*, *63*(1), 85–110.

Goldman, A. I. (2002) 'Knowledge and social norms. Review of the fate of knowledge, by H. Longino'. *Science* 296, 2148–2149

Hacking, I. (2015) 'Let's not talk about objectivity' in Padovani, F., Eichardson, H & Tsou, Y. (eds) *Objectivity in Science*. Cham:Springer

Harding, S. (1991) *Whose Science? Whose Knowledge? Thinking from Women's Lives*. Ithaca: Cornell University Press

Harding, S. (2015) *Objectivity and diversity*. University of Chicago Press

Hawley, K. (2014) 'Trust, distrust and commitment'. *Noûs*, *48*(1), 1–20.

Hicks, D. (2011) 'Is Longino's conception of objectivity feminist?' *Hypatia*, *26*(2), 333–351

Holman, B., & Geislar, S. (2018) 'Sex drugs and corporate ventriloquism: how to evaluate science policies intended to manage industry-funded bias'. *Philosophy of Science*, *85*(5), 869–881

Intemann, K. (2011) 'Diversity and dissent in science: Does democracy always serve feminist aims?' in *Feminist Epistemology and Philosophy of Science*. Springer, Dordrecht, pp. 111–132

Intergovernmental Panel on Climate Change (IPCC). (1998) 'Principles governing IPCC work'. <https://archive.ipcc.ch/pdf/ipcc-principles/ipcc-principles.pdf>

Irzik, G., & Kurtulmus, F. (2019) 'What is epistemic public trust in science?' *The British Journal for the Philosophy of Science*, *70*(4), 1145–1166

Janack, M. (2002) 'Dilemmas of objectivity'. *Social Epistemology*, *16*(3), 267–281.

Jeffrey, Richard (1956) 'Valuation and acceptance of scientific hypotheses'. *Philosophy of Science, 23*(3), 237–246

John, S. (2015) 'The example of the IPCC does not vindicate the Value Free Ideal: a reply to Gregor Betz'. *European Journal for Philosophy of Science, 5*(1), 1–13

John, S. (2018) 'Epistemic trust and the ethics of science communication: Against transparency, openness, sincerity and honesty'. *Social Epistemology, 32*(2), 75–87

John, S. (2019) 'Science, truth and dictatorship: Wishful thinking or wishful speaking?' *Studies in History and Philosophy of Science Part A, 78*, 64–72.

Jukola, S. (2015) 'Meta-analysis, ideals of objectivity, and the reliability of medical knowledge'. *Science & Technology Studies*

Kitcher, P. (1990) *The Advancement of Science*. Oxford: Oxford University Press

Koskinen, I. (2018) 'Defending a risk account of scientific objectivity'. *The British Journal for the Philosophy of Science*

Kuhn, T. (1962) *The Structure of Scientific Revolutions*. Chicago, IL: University of Chicago Press

Kuhn, T. (1977) 'Objectivity, value judgment, and theory choice' in Kuhn, T.S., (ed), *The Essential Tension – Selected Studies in Scientific Tradition and Change*. The University of Chicago Press, Chicago

Kukla, R. (2012) '"Author TBD": Radical collaboration in contemporary bio-medical research' *Philosophy of Science, 79*(5), 845–858

Kuo, L. (2019) 'China's leaders seeking to 'draw strength from weakness' in 2020'. *The Guardian* 28 Dec 2019 www.theguardian.com/world/2019/dec/28/chinas-leaders-seeking-to-draw-strength-from-weakness-in-2020

Lacey, H. (2005) *Is Science Value-Free?* London: Routledge

Levi, I. (1960) 'Must the scientist make value judgments?' *Journal of Philosophy, 57*, 345–357

Lewens, T. (2016) *The Meaning of Science: An Introduction to the Philosophy of Science*. London: Hachette UK

Lloyd, E.A. (1995) 'Objectivity and the double standard for feminist epistemologies'. *Synthese, 104*(3), 351–381

Lloyd, E.A. (1998) *The Structure and Confirmation of Evolutionary Theory*. Princeton, NJ: Princeton University Press

Lloyd, E.A. (2005) *The Case of the Female Orgasm: Bias in the Science of Evolution*. Cambridge, MA: Harvard University Press

Longino, H. (1990) *Science as Social Knowledge* Princeton, NJ: Princeton University Press

Longino, H. (1996) 'Cognitive and Non-Cognitive Values in Science: Rethinking the Dichotomy', in Nelson L.H. and Nelson J. (eds) *Feminism, Science and the Philosophy of Science*. Dordrecht: Kluwer, 39–58

Longino, H (2002) *The Fate of Knowledge*. Princeton, NJ: Princeton University Press

Longino, H (2013) *Studying Human Behaviour*. Princeton, NJ: Princeton University Press

Ludwig, D. (2015) 'Ontological Choices and the Value-Free Ideal'. *Erkenntnis*, *81*(6), 1–20.

Mackie, J.L. (1977) *Ethics: Inventing Right and Wrong*. London: Penguin Books

McMullin, E. (1982) 'Values in science'. *PSA: Proceedings of the Biennial Meeting of the Philosophy of Science Association*, *2*, 3–28

Megill, A. (1994) 'Introduction: Four Senses of Objectivity' in Megill, A. (ed) *Rethinking Objectivity*. Durham: Duke.

Menzies, P., & Price, H. (1993) 'Causation as a secondary quality'. *The British Journal for the Philosophy of Science*, *44*(2), 187–203

Nagel, T. (1986) *The View From Nowhere*. New York, NY: Oxford University Press

Nozick, R. (2001) *Invariances*. Cambridge, MA: Harvard University Press

Peters, U. (2020) 'Illegitimate Values, Confirmation Bias, and Mandevillian Cognition in Science'. *The British Journal for the Philosophy of Science*, www.journals.uchicago.edu/doi/full/10.1093/bjps/axy079

Planck, M.K. (1950) *Scientific Autobiography and Other Papers*. New York: Philosophical Library

Porter, T. (1994) *Trust in Numbers*. Princeton, NJ: Princeton University Press

Proctor, R.N. (2001) 'Commentary: Schairer and Schöniger's forgotten tobacco epidemiology and the Nazi quest for racial purity'. *International Journal of Epidemiology*, *30*(1), 31–34

Railton, P. (1984, January) 'Marx and the Objectivity of Science'. *PSA: Proceedings of the Biennial Meeting of the Philosophy of Science Association*, *2*, 813–826

Reiss, J. and Sprenger, J. (2017) 'Scientific objectivity' in Zalta E.N. (ed) *The Stanford Encyclopedia of Philosophy* (Winter 2017 Edition), https://plato.stanford.edu/archives/win2017/entries/scientific-objectivity/

Rudner, R. (1953) 'The scientist *qua* scientist makes value judgments'. *Philosophy of Science*, *20*(1), 1–6

Schickore, J. (2008) 'Doing science, writing science'. *Philosophy of Science*, *75*(3), 323–343

Schroeder, S.A. (2017) 'Using democratic values in science: an objection and (partial) response'. *Philosophy of Science, 84*(5), 1044–1054

Seaman, A. (2019) 'We need a grown-up debate about climate change'. *Spiked Online* 29 April 2019, www.spiked-online.com/2019/04/29/we-need -a-grown-up-debate-about-climate-change/

Sen, A. (2009) *The Idea of Justice* Cambridge, MA: Harvard University Press

Solomon, M. (1994) 'Social empiricism'. *Nous, 28*(3), 325–343

Solomon, M. (2007) *Social Empiricism*. Oxford: Oxford University Press

Steel, D. (2010) 'Epistemic values and the argument from inductive risk'. *Philosophy of Science, 77*(1), 14–34

Stegenga, J. (2011) 'Is meta-analysis the platinum standard?' *Studies in History and Philosophy of Biological and Biomedical Sciences, 42*(2011), 497–507

Steele, K. (2012) 'The scientist qua policy advisor makes value judgments'. *Philosophy of Science, 79*(5), 893–904

Wilholt, T. (2009) 'Bias and values in scientific research'. *Studies in History and Philosophy of Science Part A, 40*(1), 92–101

Wilholt, T. (2012) 'Epistemic trust in science'. *British Journal for the Philosophy of Science, 64*, 233–253

Williams, B. (1985) *Ethics and the Limits of Philosophy*. London: Fontana

Wright, J. (2018) 'Rescuing objectivity: A Contextualist proposal'. *Philosophy of the Social Sciences, 48*(4), 385–406

Wylie, A. (2003) 'Why Standpoint Matters', in Figueroa R. and Harding S. (eds), *Science and Other Cultures: Issues in Philosophies of Science and Technology*. New York, NY and London: Routledge, pp. 26–48

Wynne, B. (1996) 'May the sheep safely graze? A reflexive view of the expert–lay knowledge divide' in Lash, S., Szerszynski, B. & Wynne, B. (eds) *Risk, Environment and Modernity: Towards a New Ecology*. London: SAGE

Wray, K.B. (1999) 'A defense of Longino's social epistemology'. *Philosophy of Science, 66*, S538–S552.

Zammito, J. (2004) *A nice derangement of epistemes* Chicago, IL:University of Chicago Press

Cambridge Elements ≡

Philosophy of Science

Jacob Stegenga
University of Cambridge

Jacob Stegenga is a Reader in the Department of History and Philosophy of Science at the University of Cambridge. He has published widely on fundamental topics in reasoning and rationality and philosophical problems in medicine and biology. Prior to joining Cambridge, he taught in the United States and Canada, and he received his PhD from the University of California San Diego.

About the series

This series of Elements in Philosophy of Science provides an extensive overview of the themes, topics and debates which constitute the philosophy of science. Distinguished specialists provide an up-to-date summary of the results of current research on their topics, as well as offering their own take on those topics and drawing original conclusions.

Cambridge Elements ☰

Philosophy of Science

Printed in the United States
by Baker & Taylor Publisher Services